Patti Miller was raised on a farm in central western NSW and has worked teaching writing for over twenty years. Her many books include *Writing Your Life* (Allen & Unwin, 1994, 2001), *The Last One Who Remembers* (Allen & Unwin, 1997), *Child* (Allen & Unwin, 1998), *Whatever the Gods Do* (Random House, 2003) and *The Memoir Book* (Allen & Unwin, 2007). In 2012 she is teaching at the innovative Faber Academy in Sydney.

PATTI MILLER

The Mind of a Thief

UQP

First published 2012 by University of Queensland Press
PO Box 6042, St Lucia, Queensland 4067 Australia
Reprinted 2013 (three times), 2014 (twice)

www.uqp.com.au
uqp@uqp.uq.edu.au

Cataloguing-in-Publication entry is available
from the National Library of Australia
http://catalogue.nla.gov.au/

978 0 7022 4936 5 (pbk)
978 0 7022 4818 4 (ePDF)
978 0 7022 4819 1 (ePub)
978 0 7022 4820 7 (kindle)

Author photograph by Sally Flegg
Map on page ix by MAPgraphics Pty Ltd, Brisbane
Typeset in 12/17 pt Bembo by Post Pre-press Group, Brisbane
Printed in Australia by McPherson's Printing Group

University of Queensland Press uses papers that are natural, renewable
and recyclable products made from wood grown in sustainable
forests. The logging and manufacturing processes conform to
the environmental regulations of the country of origin.

For
Connie Miller
who was more inclined to read than work
1921–2010

Contents

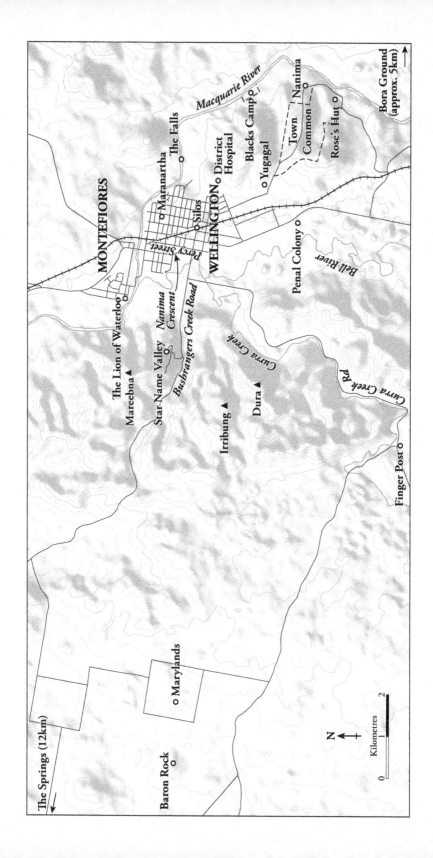

The Springs (12km)

Baron Rock ○

○ Maryland

N

Kilometres
0   1   2

MONTEFIORES

The Lion of Waterloo

Mareebna ▲

Star-Name Valley

Nanima Crescent

Bushrangers Creek Road

Iribung ▲

Dura ▲

Curra Creek

Curra Creek Rd

Finger Post ○

Maranartha ○

The Falls ○

Silos ○

Perry Street

WELLINGTON

District Hospital ○

Penal Colony ○

Bell River

Macquarie River

Blacks Camp ○

Yugagal ○

Town

Nanima ○
Common

Rose's Hut ○

Bora Ground
(approx. 5km)

1

Blackfellas

'D'ya have any blackfella in ya?' The skinny woman across the
room looked directly at me.

I was at a gathering of Wiradjuri women elders in Wellington, the country town on the central western plains of
New South Wales where I grew up. It was a while ago now,
because my mother still lived in her own house a few streets
away. The other women, standing around the table with their
cups of tea and biscuits, stopped chatting and listened. It was
their regular meeting at the Aboriginal Health Centre and
they had been discussing the usual problems: drug and alcohol addiction, violence, sexual abuse, heart disease. It seemed
every woman there had one family member, or more, struggling with at least one of the problems, but they laughed and
swapped stories as they attended to business. I was a ring-in
from the city; I'd offered to help them write their stories and
so the elders had suggested I come up to talk to them first.
They had been amiable and listened politely as I outlined how

it might work; now business had finished and they were waiting. The woman's question felt like a trap of some kind but
not too dangerous.

'No,' I said. 'Not as far as I know.'

I was aware of my accent falling into the flatter, broader
sounds of my childhood. It always happened, an automatic
adjustment towards the person I was talking to; it slipped
either way, posh or broad. It bothered me. I couldn't even
hold onto my own accent.

The skinny woman grinned and everyone who was listening chuckled. Cups were put down on saucers and arms were
folded. It was clear they all knew what she was getting at and
they were preparing to have a bit of fun with me. Despite my
family's long history here, I was an outsider. I'd been away too
long. And even though I had grown up in this district on a
farm only twenty kilometres away, none of the women looked
familiar to me. I suppose people change after twenty-five years.

They were still waiting. It was still my turn.

'Why? Do you know something I don't?'

The woman grinned again, her eyes sparkling with the
mischievous look of someone who likes to stir. She was in
her forties, about the same age as I was, dark-haired and
dark-skinned.

'Don't ask me,' she said. 'Ask Joyce Williams, Bill Riley's
sister.'

She pointed to an older woman with curly grey hair, small
and neat, the only one I'd thought looked interested when I
spoke during the meeting. I had met her brother several years
ago. Bill had come to see me at my mother's house when he
heard I was looking for someone to tell me local Aboriginal

stories. I was researching childhood stories and was looking for the ones I hadn't heard, the Aboriginal tales of how the hills and rivers and rocky outcrops were brought into being. Bill was a great storyteller.

I had found Bill in a roundabout way through my youngest brother, Terry, who used to have an Aboriginal girlfriend and played in the Aboriginal cricket team. Terry was accepted as one of them, I'm not sure why. Perhaps it's because he has always had a 'watching from the edge' air about him, aware of, but not really part of, the busy world. One of the Aboriginal men I talked to had said, 'Terry's just like an Aborigine, worse sometimes'. And then he laughed.

The women watched me as I circled around the narrow crowded room towards Joyce. The Health Centre was in an old corner shop, a nest of different-sized rooms freshly painted and fitted out, but still poky. I had to push past several chairs, which made a scraping noise as they slid on the floor. It was mid morning and already hot in the closed-in room. I felt sweat trickling under my black top.

'The others reckon I should ask you if I have any Aboriginal in me.'

Joyce looked at me shrewdly. 'The whitefellas and the blackfellas have two different stories about who's related to who in this town.'

The other women burst out laughing. I stood there feeling like an unwilling clown. I hate not knowing what everyone else knows.

'Ya dad's Don Miller.'

It was more a statement than a question so I just nodded. There were dozens of Millers in Wellington, not all of us related. It didn't even occur to me until later to be surprised that Joyce, a woman I'd never met before, knew who I was, who my father was, who I was related to.

'Ya heard of ya dad's grandma, Rosina May?'

Of course I'd heard of her. My father used to tell us about visiting her smoky, dirt-floored hut when he was a boy. He always said she was 'a blackfella', but we didn't really believe him because he always grinned when he said it.

'Well, my grandfather was John May, Rosina's brother. Ya dad's grandma and my grandad are brother an' sister. So me an' you, we're cousins.'

Now it was my turn to grin. I'm as red-haired and freckle-faced as they come. There's no way I would have imagined I had Aboriginal ancestors. I could hear my heart beating.

'But I think Rosina's parents came out from England. They must have been white. If we're cousins we must be related through the white side,' I countered.

'Don't you remember how dark ya pop was?'

It was true; Dad's father, Frank, did have dark skin. He and my grandmother, Emily, had bought a house in town after they handed the farm on to their youngest son. The oldest son, Donald, my father, already had his farm, bought from an uncle, so he didn't need any help. The house in town had a big yard where Granny Miller grew roses, sweet peas, poppies, pansies and snow-on-the-mountain out the front and vegetables out the back. She was a renowned gardener and must have luxuriated in being able keep her garden thriving with 'town water' every day. My pop watched her work from the veranda, digging, weeding, raking. I don't recall him ever doing any-thing except sitting and watching. Now I remembered that even in the winter, sitting hunched in his chair with a rug on his knees, his face and hands were dark. I felt a quick thrill of excitement.

'And what about Kevin and Dickie Miller?' the skinny woman chimed in. 'Especially Dickie. You only have to look at 'im.'

Kevin and Dick were my second cousins, several years older than me. They were both shearers, working in our shed some years. While they were shearing they wore blue dungarees and singlets and their arm muscles were sweaty and sometimes streaked with oil from the shearing machinery. They both seemed a bit dangerous. Dick, especially, had a reputation for being wild. I remembered his large features and dark skin and his defiant, handsome 'bad boy' air.

'Ask Claudia what she reckons,' said the woman. 'You know Claudia, Dickie's wife, dontcha?' She indicated a large, soft-looking black woman standing to the back of the group. I had never seen her before, my own cousin's wife.

'Hallo,' I said, embarrassed.

She answered shyly, clearly unwilling to be part of the game. She looked at me quickly then looked away to the woman who had started the conversation.

I turned back to Joyce. 'So where did they come from, the Mays?'

'Here. Wellington. Just out by Guerie, you know.'

That rang a bell. My father had done some family research at one stage, as people often do, and I recalled there was a Guerie connection. A large door to the past seemed to be swinging open; I felt a mounting surge of delight and uncertainty but tried to hide my excitement.

'And John May was your grandfather and Rosina's brother?'

'Yeah, that's what I said.'

'Was he dark or white?'

'He was pretty light. Not as dark as Rosina. She was dark.'

'But they were proper brother and sister?'

'Yeah, yeah.'

A bit impatient with me now. The other women started talking to each other again. The game was already over.

Joyce turned and introduced me to a young Aboriginal woman who had just come in. She worked at the Health Centre and was her granddaughter, I think, but I'm not sure of that now. 'This is my cousin Patti.'

I shook her hand, blushing. Was it true? Whites claiming dubious Aboriginal ancestry had always irritated me. Joyce shouldn't accept me so easily; I'm just a nosy ring-in. And so damn white it was silly. I want to have Aboriginal ancestry – who wouldn't want to be connected to 40,000 years of lineage in their homeland? – but to look at I'm still as pale as my original European ancestors. At the same time, I couldn't keep the smile off my face as Joyce kept introducing me as her cousin. What if the ancient line of Wiradjuri blood did flow in my veins? What if some of my ancestors really had strode long-legged through the bush, danced in fire-lit corroborees, slept under the stars for tens of thousands of years right here in this place where I was born? A deep longing pulsed somewhere in the region of my heart, irrational perhaps, but irresistible.

Maybe there was a Wiradjuri woman waiting in the past for me, but would that change who I was? Would I have a different identity?

2

Wiradjuri Land

As a child, I didn't know I was growing up on Wiradjuri land. I lived on Marylands, a wheat and sheep farm near Wellington, about 250 miles from Sydney. We called Wellington 'town' and we drove there to buy groceries, to go to St Patrick's church and for my five brothers to play cricket. The Western Stores dominated the main street, along with the sturdy nineteenth-century banks, the Greek milk bar and Cameron Park. The other side of the park followed the curves of the Bell River which flowed into the Macquarie, itself beginning as a stream in the mountains near Bathurst and flowing all the way up through the Macquarie Marshes to the Darling, which eventually entered the sea near Adelaide more than a thousand kilometres away. I knew my geography but I didn't know the land these rivers flowed through was Wiradjuri. I hadn't even heard the word.

The names of tribes, or nations, were not taught at school in those days; only Aborigines existed. Aborigines had lived on our property in the olden days. I learned this at the one-room school up the road from our farm, but my father had also found evidence. One day when he was walking across the back paddock he came upon two stone axes. One of them was of a reddish brown stone and roughly made. The other was grey and smooth, with a perfectly sharp edge. I loved to hold it and was very proud of it, partly because it gave me some status to have such a good specimen for Social Studies, but also, I suspect, because I had the idea that Aborigines weren't impressive compared to the Chinese or Egyptians or anyone else we learned about, and I was relieved that they could make something so beautiful and so skilfully shaped.

I admired our Albert Namitjira paintings – I didn't know they were prints – on the wall at school too. Even my grandmother had a Namitjira picture in her house in town; he was popular in the early sixties. I loved the purpling haze of hills and the white trunks of the gum trees and the red earth – and most of all that a real Aborigine had painted them. I don't remember seeing any traditional Aboriginal art, except photographs in a schoolbook of historical bark paintings and of body painting, which my brothers tried to copy with white paint on their faces and chests.

My brothers and sisters and I played at being Aborigines just as we played Cowboys and Indians: building gunyahs or mia-mias out of sticks and bark; digging up fat white grubs with orange heads and daring each other to eat them; making spears and bull-roarers; practising our tracking skills. I especially wanted to be a tracker. Being able to follow an animal or person days after they had passed by noting the faint mark of their paw or foot print was impressive enough, but observing such tiny changes as a bent blade of grass or broken twig suggested extraordinary powers. There were lots of tracks for us to practise on: each other's bare footprints, perky magpie scribblings, solid clumpy cattle hooves, the neat semicircle of a horse's hoof, small, delicate sheep hooves – although sheep, to our continuing surprise, would all trot one behind the other for years on end, making deep paths across the farm, easy to follow and most useful if we had to walk through a paddock of Bathurst burrs or prickly grasses.

Sometimes we made our own tracks: bird claw prints with sticks, or snake tracks by twisting the side of the foot on fine dust. The skill was in beginning and ending the track subtly enough to convince, for the point of this whole painstaking exercise was to fool a younger brother or sister into believing there was a snake nearby. Being in the middle of eight kids, fifth from the top, I was both tricked and a 'tricker', as we called it. There was great annoyance in being tricked, and great glee in being a successful tricker, but if our mother or father were told, we had to confess and take the consequences of making up stories.

By the time I was ten or eleven, I had started making up stories at night for my younger sister, Mary, with whom I shared the front room. Our room must have been the living room originally as the front door of the house opened straight into it and it had a fireplace and mantelpiece, but it had been a bedroom for all our family's time. Its walls were made of smooth vertical slabs of wood, too thick to be called boards, between which I could see sunlight glittering if I was in bed during the day. It was too cold in winter and too hot in summer, part of a poor settler's house built for English conditions with the addition of lino since then, and lilac paint. We slept without sheets in the winter, preferring the cosy prickle of woollen blankets to the icy feel of cotton, although when I think of it now, it probably was also that we didn't have enough sheets to go around in the winter when the washing could be flapping wet on the line for a few days. In summer, we lay outside on blankets under the stars and told stories until it was cool enough to go inside.

My sister was dark-eyed and brown-skinned and looked like a bush Aborigine with her bird's nest tangle of sun-bleached hair, a complete contrast to my red hair and freckles. I would often find her sitting on the back step, staring dreamily into another world, which irritated me because I didn't have access to wherever she was. At the same time, she was agile and a fast runner on her thin wiry legs – the fastest for her age in the district with bundles of blue ribbons from the sports days to prove it. In bed at night, she was the perfect listener, completely entering into the stories I invented, which were often serial fables about the moon and stars or instructional tales such as the life cycle of a drop of water, suitably personified with its own character traits. Once, for months, the story was the adventures of two Aboriginal children. I loved telling this story. Forty years later, I still remember the central characters' names, Aruma and Allarie, which I found in a *Women's Weekly* article on Aboriginal words.

I chronicled the children's daily lives: hunting possums and lizards, catching fish, collecting seeds and witchetty grubs, making little boomerangs, lighting fires with two sticks and – each night at the close of the story – snuggling up under their kangaroo skin rugs by the fire. Allarie, the girl, was older than her brother, Aruma, and consequently spent quite a bit of time explaining how to track kangaroos and emus and goannas, as well as how to make coolamons, nulla-nullas and boomerangs. They lived on either the banks of the nearby Little River, or the Macquarie, which ran through Wellington; I can't remember which, but they were definitely on a river because I knew they would need a water supply. On the farm there was a creek, which only flowed after heavy rain, and two waterholes, both too small and muddy to drink from or catch anything other than yabbies. Once, Aruma and Allarie walked across our land, on a long day's chase after a honey bee. They climbed one of our gum trees and played in our creek and drank a little of the muddy water because they were so thirsty.

One night I thought of the most exciting story-line with the most thrilling conclusion ever. I was so excited I nearly told Mary immediately. But I already knew most of the pleasure was in the withholding, so I kept it to myself and started telling the story.

The children had heard about the sea from other Aborigines who had 'gone walkabout' and passed through their camp, but they had never seen it. They wondered if it was true and longed to see it for themselves. They longed in the same way that my sisters and brothers and I did, with the same passionate, almost hopeless but unrelenting desire that only children can have for something that is not in their power to attain. I had seen the sea when I was seven, three or four years back, before the long drought that took up the rest of my childhood and it had become the site of mythic, never-to-be-repeated joy. It was easy to know exactly how Allarie and Aruma felt.

Their desire was so strong that they started making secret plans to set out across the dry rolling plains, across the far mountains and all the way over hundreds of miles to the sea.

I stretched the story out, mile by mile, detailing the children's every adventure along the way; how Aruma caught his first goanna, how sometimes they could find nothing to eat and lay down tired and hungry, how they were threatened by snakes and by an evil witchdoctor who was going to 'point the bone' at them, how they slept in caves, how they saw the Three Sisters in the Blue Mountains, how they smelled the salt of the sea from fifty miles away just like we did. And then I slowed it down even more, so that they slept the night in the tussocky grass on the side of a high sand dune, not realising the sea was on the other side. I stopped the story there for that night. The next day, I had them wake up, stretch, light a fire and cook the magpie they had caught earlier. Not until then did I let them climb the sand dune and there, lo and behold, were eleven huge white birds, each a thousand times bigger than any bird they had even seen, bobbing gently on a vast, all-the-way-to-the-sky, blue and green sea.

'Although they didn't know the date, not having this way of measuring time,' I said portentously, 'it was the twenty-sixth of January, 1788.'

I don't recall if Mary was as thrilled as I thought she should be, but I remember my own pleasure in bringing about such an unexpected (I thought) and satisfying conclusion.

3

Identity Terror

After the Wiradjuri elders' meeting in Wellington, I went
back to my mother's place where I was staying. Her brick
Federation house was much bigger than she needed, but when
they sold the farm my parents had wanted enough rooms to
fit their eight children in whenever they might come home
to visit. Dad had died since, so it was just my mother, and on
occasion, brief floods of children and grandchildren. She said
she felt silly there by herself.

I sat down at the formica table in the kitchen and told her
about our new relations. I was the privileged bearer of news
about our family. We were not who we thought we were; we
had a richer and more interesting story than anyone knew. We
were from deep in this ground; we belonged.

My mother didn't seem that surprised. 'It's what your dad
always said.'

'I know, but we thought he was joking. This is different.
Joyce is an elder. She's claiming us.'

Mum shrugged. It wasn't that unusual to have Aborigines in the family; my eldest brother had married a woman of Aboriginal background and they had four beautiful daughters before they divorced, and my youngest brother lived with his Aboriginal girlfriend for two years and brought up her baby daughter as his own before she left for Queensland. Both women were Wiradjuri; we were already related.

'Gran Miller wouldn't have liked it,' my mother offered.

'What do you mean? Didn't she like Aborigines?'

The Millers weren't 'flash'. I couldn't see what Gran had to feel superior about.

'She wouldn't have any of that sort of talk. That they were related to the Mays.'

'What? You mean she knew. Why weren't we told?'

'Don always said it,' my mother defended.

'Yeah, but he also said he stole you from the blackfellas.'

My mother smiled. It was a reference to her mass of unruly black hair, part of a set of stories about my parents and their cherishing of each other. My father was a religious man, and anxious, but when it came to my mother he was affectionate and playful, even in his declining years. Once, during the last few months when he sometimes didn't recognise his family, my mother, her black hair streaked with grey, asked him, 'Do you know who I am?' and he answered, 'Yes, you're the one with the stripy hair.'

She talked then about my father instead. I had heard all of her stories about him before, dozens of times, but it didn't matter. They were like a colour wash over my own memories, strengthening the dye. I let them soak in, tinting my set of images of parents who loved each other, a little rosier and simpler than could be natural, in retrospect, but my mother's stories affirmed the original colours must have been warm and fast.

My mother and I didn't talk about it again that day, but later I did tell my brothers and sisters of the possible Wiradjuri ancestor Joyce had revealed. It was the first echo of Dad's story we had heard. My youngest brother said he always felt as if the place was speaking to him and my younger sister remembered her dreamy sense of another reality. Everyone liked the possibility of having an Aboriginal ancestor; it seemed a mark of unquestionable belonging in this country. No-one knew if it was true or not, and since nothing appeared to have been recorded, there was probably no way of finding out. On record, Rosina's father was Charles May and her mother was either Lauannah or Lavinia Chew – which sounds as if she could have been Chinese – but she was supposed to have been born in England. Maybe that was fiction. Maybe she was a local Wiradjuri woman.

I tried to imagine her. Perhaps she was gentle and shy like my father, or wild and unpredictable like Dickie Miller. Probably slender and short as most of my family is. It was impossible to know the facts. I thought about her more as an image, a poetic idea, a young woman sitting cross-legged in the shade under a river gum, changing the course of my family's history, connecting me to the Dreamtime. It was seductive, the longed for communion with this place.

But then I wondered how much my ancestry and history really made me who I am. Did it make any difference if she was truly Wiradjuri or not? How much do these stories of our individual and communal pasts make any of us? They are tales re-told by family or history books, highly selective if not, at times, imaginary. Hair and skin colour and health are inherited, but culture and stories are re-told in the moment. The warp and weft of identity is re-woven every time and is so tightly and thickly made it seems we were born with it, part of our flesh, instead of it being only a cloak.

I didn't keep in touch with Joyce. I meant to. For several months afterwards, up to a year or so, it seemed likely that I would call in and see her whenever I went up to Wellington to visit my mother. By the second year it seemed possible, but not really likely, and then, finally, I knew I wouldn't do it. Joyce would have forgotten me, I had lost her phone number, she might not even be alive anymore, we might not be related anyway, my mother needed more attention these days; there are always plenty of reasons not to stay in touch.

In this time things had changed in their natural irrevocable way. My mother had had a stroke and had to move to Mara-nartha, the retirement unit in Wellington. She could still walk and talk, wash herself and get dressed and make a cup of tea – and make her dry political comments – but her peripheral vision was gone. On the edge of her vision there was only absence. Because the mind does not comprehend absence it invented things to put there and so my mother saw castles in paddocks along the road. She knew they weren't there and was well aware they were visual hallucinations. She only wryly complained that she would have thought her mind would come up with something a bit more sensible than castles to fill in the gaps.

The loss of peripheral vision made it difficult for her to

do cryptic crosswords and to read, her two principal remaining pleasures, but with some retraining and a great deal of effort, she did manage to decipher words, coping with the annoyance of losing the beginning and ending of lines with a modicum of grace.

Her limited sight also affected her ability to find her way about. It is extraordinary how much we rely on what we can see on the edges of our vision to make our way around with any confidence. All kinds of information about the fringes of our world are registered and processed, enabling us to step out along the footpath or across the street. My mother's sense of direction, like mine, was never good so it seemed simply an exaggeration of her natural propensity that she got lost in the retirement unit.

At the same time, I had also begun to lose my way. It wasn't dramatic, just a slow dissolving of what had seemed solid. My sons had both left home and my partner, Anthony, and I had moved from the Blue Mountains to a lively street in Kings Cross, the frantic faltering heart of the city. It might seem a perverse instinct to move to the chaos of a city when children are grown; tranquillity and natural beauty are usually more appealing to me. But children had connected me noisily to my community and when they left there was a chilly silence in our tree-filled backyard. I longed for the sound of voices and footsteps, for things being arranged, things being dropped, picked up, tidied, left lying around. I wanted cries, shouts, laughter, arguments, mess, glances, conversations in many languages; I wanted the endlessly various stream of humanity to pass my front door. I wanted my space and time filled up, jam-packed. To hold me in place. And so we moved.

The problem was, it wasn't really working. My life was jam-packed, but nothing I did or said felt necessary. The nearest I can come to describing it is that I wasn't convinced by myself. I knew well enough that a self is made; I had read just enough eastern philosophy and contemporary neuroscience to be persuaded it was all a construction, a flickering of electrical impulses. I could even sit down if I had nothing better to do and list what I was made of – memories, books, imaginings, relationships – it's just that I could see and feel the vast emptiness under the construction too clearly. I wasn't terrified, nor panicked, just desolate. I suspected there must be a biological component to the feeling of no ground beneath my feet, that the loss of the ability to create new life must have left a vast space; but the fact is the space had always been there and it had opened up before.

Years ago, when I had two young children and was immersed in the bread and honey of life, I went through a period of what might be called identity terror. It was a time of my life I've tried to understand before. During those months I would lie on my bed – it always began when I was lying down – and what felt like a steel band would start to form around my skull. It didn't matter if I asked to be held, or if I jumped up and walked around the house, or strode out into the wild garden, or tried to read or watch television, once the tightening began, the panic would always follow.

The absurd thing was, there was nothing in my life to be anxious about. I was young, not yet thirty. I had – still have – a soul mate, Anthony, who was passionate about the life of art. I had two beautiful sons, a room of my own for writing, and with a little care, money for a week or two in a sprawling share house by the seaside each summer. I breathed in the shimmering pale indigo haze of eucalypts above ochre cliffs; I planted a waratah in memory of my father; I had Sunday lunch with friends on the veranda. Admittedly, I was exhausted from a couple of years of being woken at night by a restless child, but I thought I was managing.

And yet the panic came and, for what seemed like a long time, stayed.

It began literally overnight. That first time, I was on a mattress on my friend Merril's lounge-room floor in Canberra. After dinner and the usual long conversation with Merril, I went to bed my ordinary, cheerful enough self and woke up at around two, panic-stricken. I had not been dreaming but was suddenly wide awake. I couldn't see anything except for the dim shapes of furniture but I knew something fundamental was missing. My heart thumped as I stared into the darkness. It took some time to realise what was gone; somehow, terrifyingly, *nothing had meaning* anymore.

I got up and felt my way to the kitchen and filled a glass with water and drank it. Water is good for all sorts of ailments; the feel of the cold liquid going down my throat might wake whichever part of my brain created meaning.

I sternly advised myself that, in the morning, all would be as it always had been. I lay awake for hours, feeling the thumping of my heart and the panic and then slept for an hour or two before dawn. When I woke to the early morning light, my throat was dry despite the noisy water I had drunk in the night. And the fear was still there.

I told Merril what had happened. Astonishingly, she

appeared to know what I was talking about. So this happens to other people, I thought. That made me feel better – I am not one of those people who wants to be unique, especially not in suffering.

We went out walking across a nearby park. I remember a slope of grass, dotted gums, manuka, glittering sunlight in cold wintery air. I could see that it was beautiful, but it did not move me or touch me in any way. I had always depended on beauty. Overnight it deserted me.

Afterwards Merril tucked me into bed, put on a Bach CD, instructed me to breathe. She told my boys I was not feeling well. I lay there wondering how long meaning was going to abandon me.

It lasted in varying degrees of intensity for the rest of winter, into the spring and the summer. A few times, not more than two or three, a new terror arrived. The first time it sprang again out of the dark; I was lying in my own bed with Anthony next to me and should have felt as safe and content as any person could feel, but instead I woke and knew that not only had the world around me lost meaning, but my entire identity had dissolved. I had no boundaries; I was as vast as the universe but I was made of nothing except fear. I had read that having no sense of self was a liberation, the end point of the spiritual path, but this could not be what was meant. My self was dispersed, whatever glue that held me together had dissolved.

Still, over those months when I wrote or read, I felt quite normal; the world melded itself back together and the anxiety abated. I can see now the fact that I could read and write means that I was not in as severe a state as I thought. But I had not experienced tremors and shocks of the mind before and so had nothing to compare them to.

It would be easy to argue it was all a product of nervous exhaustion, of not enough sleep, but to me that is beside the point. The point is why do neurones give up on the job of creating meaning when they are tired? Why do they give up on the story of self as if it was all a fiction anyway? At times it makes me wonder if there is anything solid about me at all – or about anyone else.

And then, for months, sometimes years on end, I have not given it a thought. I have been too busy to even notice what I am made of. When I met Joyce for the first time and she told me we were related, it was a period when I was rooted deep in my life, immersed in work and family. The details of my sense of self had proliferated and solidified since that weird split in my late twenties. It was years ago, that dissolved feeling. Her offer of another identity was exciting and attractive; I could feel my blood leaping towards it, but it seemed superfluous. At that time it was a gift I didn't need.

4

Dreaming

Early one morning in my flat in Kings Cross, I had a dream with no storyline, not even any images, just a muttered sentence. The sentence wasn't dramatic or symbolic, simply a low voice saying, 'Go back to the town you came from and tell its story'.

I woke abruptly. Tell what bloody story? Wellington is a five-hour drive north-west of Sydney, a town of 4000 people and falling, five pubs, two cafés, two supermarkets, one swimming pool, no picture theatre. Where was the story?

I lay in bed for a while feeling resentful. Anthony was still asleep beside me, softly hunching the sheets around his shoulder as I rolled over.

I didn't even come from town. I grew up twenty kilometres west. I bought musk stick lollies at Kimbell's Tea Rooms in town on Saturday mornings and I swam at the town baths in summer. I went to the convent high school in Percy Street for four years, in and out every day on the bus. I was allowed to go down the street to buy groceries for home from the Western Stores if I had a note. Wellington was a town of about 6000 people in the heyday of the late sixties – a small cluster of Federation homes, some pretty cottages, a few Housing Commission fibro places, lots of rose gardens. The streets gathered around the wheat silos towering like ziggurats by the railway line. But even then the town seemed slow, somehow lacking the will to get out of its own way. There was nothing much more to say about it.

Anthony stirred and then was wide awake and ready to get up in his early bird way.

'I had a dream about Wellington,' I said.

'Interesting?'

'No, it was just a sentence.'

'Sentences are useful,' he said.

As I lay there grumbling, a magpie carolled in the beech tree outside the bedroom window. The carolling of magpies always resonates with happiness for me, bringing back a precise childhood memory of lying in bed one morning during the long drought of the sixties and hearing them sing outside in the gums. The joyful carolling suddenly let me believe for a few seconds that the world outside was not desolate and parched, but green and pretty with streams running and white lambs playing like a farm in a book.

I was only ten years old, but I had already gained the idea that life in books was not only the best and most correct life, but that the more actual life could resemble life in books, the more real it was. Because most of my books were English, the poor scraggy lambs and dried-out paddocks outside in the hot morning were never going to be real, let alone correct.

But the magpie was calling again in the present so I sat up a little and peered out through the study windows to the old avocado tree. It had only seven pears on its straggly branches, perhaps its last year of fruit. In the next backyard there was a magnolia and another beech, and then angophora gums and a palm tree, all of them strangers among the old apartment blocks of the city.

I silently complained about the dream until it was time to get up. Then I looked on the internet to see what I could find out about Wellington. I'm not one to ignore a dream instruction however dull it is, especially when there is nothing else on offer.

That's when I found out that just a few months after the Mabo decision in 1993, which ruled Indigenous Australians had a natural law right to their native land, the first ever post-Mabo Native Title claim in Australia was made in my home town.

I knew immediately that this was the story my dream meant. I can't understand or defend this knowing, but there was a blind sense of having found what I was looking for. The story of my place might not tell me who I was, but if I could examine its weave, I might at least see what my cloak was made of.

That first morning I read dozens of articles online. Astonishingly, the land claim appeared to have been resolved just the day before. According to the newspapers, a parcel of land called The Town Common at Wellington had been returned under the NSW Land Rights Act to the original Native Title claimants within the last twenty-four hours. It wasn't a native title decision, but I didn't know that yet.

The timing struck me as extraordinary. It seemed too much of a coincidence to have the dream the night the claim was resolved. It was also my mother's birthday, which was unrelated, but when you're in that heightened state of discovery, everything seems to have meaning. To me at that moment, it conveyed a sense of purpose, a sense that this was indeed my story.

I had very few clues. I didn't know how the Mabo decision worked in practice; I didn't know the difference between Native Title and Aboriginal Land Rights, or why the claim had gone on for so long, nor any of the people involved. In the face of all that I didn't know, I felt overwhelmed, but there is nothing like a dream instruction and a few coincidental dates to create a fiery sense of destiny.

I wished I had kept in touch with Joyce. She wasn't mentioned in any of the articles, but her brother Bill Riley was. My mother had told me Bill had died a few years ago, but Joyce would be sure to know what had been going on. I would have to find her again.

The other name that kept appearing was Rose Chown. There were a couple of photographs of her too, an imposing-looking woman, sturdy and solid like a small monolith, perhaps in her forties, black-skinned with long straight black hair flowing down her back. I gazed at the screen. Her large dark eyes stared back in a slightly hooded way as if she didn't want the photographer to see into her. She was vice president and spokesperson for the Wellington Town Common Committee, the group that had made the land claim. According to the newspaper reports, the case had dragged on over the years, since 1993 in fact, and from the sketchy details it seemed the main reason was that there had been opposition to the claim, not from white landholders but from another Aboriginal group. And it looked like Bill Riley was a spokesperson for the other group. I was puzzled. Why was one group of Aborigines opposing another group's land claim?

Without an introduction, I was reluctant to ring anyone. Living in the middle of Kings Cross with memories of growing up in a white family on a farm near a country town didn't give me automatic permission to waltz back in and start asking questions. Besides, if there were sides then there could be conflict and I could make it worse by talking to the wrong person first. And they might well be suspicious of a strange white woman ringing them up without warning. Still, I had to ask someone and Rose seemed the obvious person to begin with.

It took me a week to track Rose down through the Aboriginal Health Centre and then I rang her quickly before I lost my nerve.

'I'm one of the Millers from out Suntop way. Out along the Yeovil Road.'

'Yeah, I know it. You turn off at Fingerpost.'

'That's it. We had a place past Suntop school. My dad has died but my mum still lives in Wellington, at Maranartha, you know, the retirement village? I live in Sydney now but I still go up there a lot.'

Having located myself in the landscape, I plunged into the dream and finding the Native Title story and asked would she help me. It didn't go so well. From this safe distance, I'm still trying to work out when the conversation first went awry. Was it when I said I wanted to hear everyone's side of the story? That was when her voice changed. Whatever Rose thought I was referring to, she was ready to deflect me.

'We don't want to hash over problems in the past with other people. And we don't want them to hash over their problems with us.'

Her voice was noticeably cooler; not defensive, but suddenly keeping me at arm's length with a tone that implied she might not talk to me at all. There was no overt conflict, no raised voice. I tried to make up the ground I'd so deftly cut from under myself.

'Of course not,' I said. 'I understand. I just want to hear the story.'

I rattled on, agreeing with everything she said, panicked that I might lose her before I'd even begun. I couldn't believe how stupid I'd been. What was I thinking, a white woman who had grown up on Rose's country, implying that Aborigines argued among themselves about who had rights to the land, so why should we believe any of them? It wasn't what I meant, but that's how it sounded. I'd probably blown my chance to talk to the woman who made the first post-Mabo Native Title claim in Australia.

I kept talking, too much and too fast. 'I just want to talk to lots of people. I'm really interested in how the Native Title claim all happened – I mean it took years, didn't it? I come up to visit my mum often. I've just been up, last weekend, and I thought I'd come up again in a couple of weeks. Maybe the first week after the New Year.'

Rose listened but I knew I wasn't making much headway. She would not commit to a time or place but she ended up agreeing that I could telephone her when I next came to Wellington to see how we got along from there.

At least, that's what *I* said. 'We'll see how we get along.'

She said, 'We'll see what transpires.'

I felt wrong-footed again, misjudging the register. Who says 'transpires'? I put the phone down. I had almost certainly blown it already. Why couldn't I have kept my mouth shut? I had only meant to suggest that I had an idea of what had been going on.

I picked my way backwards to the beginning of the phone call, trying to remember what I said after introducing myself.

'I'm interested in writing about the Wiradjuri land claim.' Direct and simple.

'So are we,' Rose had responded swiftly. 'We want our history to be written.'

Ah, there it was! Right at the beginning of the first exchange. The moment I felt the sharp tug of something being wrenched away that I had thought was mine. It was my story, I found it, it was my dream; I could see the plaintive, illogical justifications going by at the speed of light, but Rose was far too quick for me. I wasn't ready, I didn't have much of a hold on it anyway – didn't even know what I was trying to hold onto.

'Great,' I said. 'Maybe we can be of use to each other.'

Even as I said it I knew it wasn't true. Whatever I thought I was doing, I had no intention of 'being of use', of writing a history for the Wiradjuri committee or for anyone else. I am not a historian or anthropologist or ethnologist. Not even a journalist. I didn't know what I was doing or where I was heading but some dumb part of me knew I had to try to follow the muttered instructions that had come into my sleeping brain from the dark.

I couldn't give it up. I had no idea of which way to go and no compass to guide me.

I've always liked compasses. I like the look of them, especially the old-fashioned ones made of brass with a glass cover, small enough to fit into the palm of your hand. Most of all I like the extraordinarily mysterious means by which a compass works – the way its fine needle, delicately balanced, aligns itself with the north–south magnetic field of the interior of earth itself. The electrons in the magnet are pulled in line by the magnetic field of the earth, which is created by the slow whirling of the molten iron core. Even apart from the fabulous science, it strikes me as wonderful that the earth has created a means by which her inhabitants can find their way.

Of course, the Wiradjuri could find their way without compasses. Following stars and rivers and rocky hills, they navigated their way across vast tracts of land. They made pathways too, worn over millennia by traders carrying axes and arrowheads, and messengers carried carved sticks along them to arrange corroborees and battles. The bush wasn't as trackless as the Europeans thought it was, nor as unreadable, but longitude and latitude and compasses are lovely constructions and easier to interpret than landscape.

My original compass was the landscape I grew up in, the farm and a few square miles of surrounding land. Despite longing for other lands, lands that existed in books, whenever I looked at this country, I knew who I was and where I was going. I was born on this dry land, so was my father, my grand-father, my great-grandfather, my great-great-grandfather, perhaps even an ancestral Wiradjuri great-great-grandmother. I did not live in the central west after I left school, but I didn't have to. The place sang in my bones, there was no chance I would lose my way.

But I had, several times. The insubstantiality of self, says the Buddhist monk Chogyam Trungpa, is the truth of being, but I have found it a desolate place. He says the experience of self is one fleeting thought after another, which we generate fast enough to create the illusion of a continuous and solid self, a bit like the frames of a film creating the illusion of continuous movement. Despite being an inveterate collector of evidence of my continuity – memories, talismans, photo-graphs – I must have slowed down in splicing together the frames.

For years I have kept a photograph on my desk of Baron Rock, the rocky hill behind our farm. I suppose I have always known it was evidence of who I was. Geologically described, Baron Rock is a lopsided volcanic plug, weathered over mil-lions of years to a rocky outcrop surrounded by flat land and gentle undulations. There is nothing spectacular about its shape or size – although from a certain angle it has the appear-ance of a resting lion – but whenever I looked at it, I felt like a Christian gazing at the stony cave in Bethlehem, an Aborig-ine regarding Uluru. My brothers and sisters and I explored it when we wanted adventure. Its cliffs and caves and high rocky shelves offered more possibilities than the open paddocks all around us. From the high windy top we could see for miles in every direction. When I stood up there, I wondered if Aborigine kids before me had ever climbed up and looked out over the unbroken countryside and wanted something different to happen.

5

Heading Home – and Leaving

Two weeks after the dream, Anthony and I drove west out of the city to visit my mother. Before we left, I rang Rose Chown again to let her know I was coming up in the hope she might have relented and would agree to talk to me, but she didn't answer the telephone. Perhaps she was away. Each time the telephone rang out I wondered about the relief I felt.

In the Blue Mountains, which rise at the end of the suburbs, Anthony and I stopped to see an old friend. Banksias and grevilleas waved their ancient-looking fronds, their odd spiky flowers pretending to be civilised in her garden. She made us a cup of tea and we sat on her wide front veranda, catching up. I told her I had decided to write the story of the Native Title claim in my home town and its connection to my own family's history. I said was I going to interview the people who had made the claim just as soon as I could make a few contacts.

'Why should they talk to you?' she asked. It wasn't so much a question as an accusation; I was minding other people's business.

'I come from there. I'm a local,' I said, feeling defensive.

'Yes, but not for a long time. And you're not Aboriginal.'

I felt like telling her about Joyce being related to me, but it didn't feel true enough to repeat, especially since I had done nothing about it.

'But people know my family. They know who I am,' I said instead.

'Mmm.' Again it was a disapproving sound. 'You can't just turn up and expect people to talk to you.'

She had studied Aboriginal culture for years and knew what she was talking about, but there was a certain tone of possessiveness as well. It was her territory and I was trespassing, or that's what I imagined in my prickly state.

'I wasn't just going to turn up. I am going to ask around, find some contacts.' I didn't want to tell her about Rose turning me down already.

'There's a woman at Sydney Uni in the Anthropology department who might be able to help. Gaynor Macdonald. She has researched and written a lot about the Wiradjuri. I don't have her address but I am sure you could find it easily.'

'Is she Wiradjuri?'

'No, but she knows a lot. She knows how to approach people.'

I took out a piece of paper and wrote Gaynor's name on it. I didn't have enough of anything, information or contacts, to turn down any help.

We headed up the highway to Victoria Pass and wound

down the other side of the mountains towards the beginning of Wiradjuri territory.

'Still want to take this on?' Anthony asked.

A few hours later we sat in the car in Percy Street, the main street in Wellington. It's called Nanima Crescent for part of the way, but it's all the same street, lined with old shops on one side, half of them empty, and Cameron Park on the other.

'I'm sorry I came from this puddle and not an ancient hill-top village in the south of France,' I said. 'That would be more exciting.'

'It's hardly your fault.' Anthony shrugged.

We both stared out the car window. It was tiring just look-ing at the street empty of cars, the boarded-up department store, the ugly shit-yellow Bi-Lo supermarket wall where the lovely iron-laced verandas of the Royal Hotel used to be. No-one cared enough to stop it being knocked down.

No-one bothered with anything much in Wellington. My mother kept us updated with developments: the new super-market was the main topic of conversation for six months; a new jail that was going to be built on the outskirts of town by Richard Crookes (!) occupied conversation for another twelve months; then another new supermarket supplied more fuel. One quirky café opened in the old Spanish missionary style school, but it wasn't enough to change the mood of a whole town.

In Australian terms, Wellington is an old town. It celebrated its sesquicentenary when I was a teenager – I remember writing a story called 'Gold' for the Shire Council's commemorative competition. It made a symbolic parallel between finding gold near Wellington and the golden sunshine on golden wattle and the golden future. Truthfully, I didn't see or want any kind of future there, golden or otherwise. I couldn't wait to leave, feared not leaving.

Still, it's a pretty town, despite the desolate main street. It dozes around its two rivers in a valley surrounded by hills, and there are the solid Federation houses with wide verandas and rose gardens. It's just that it feels dispirited, as if life never amounted to what was promised. Even in the hopeful nineteenth century, a visitor commented in a local history book, 'stagnation is the term most appropriate to the life of the district'. The weary smell of stagnation; I think that's what I smelled as a teenager at school in Wellington and had to leave to avoid breathing it in. Now every year the population shrinks, every year there are fewer and fewer children and teenagers, more and more elderly women like my mother struggling slowly along the footpath past the empty shops towards the gaudy supermarket. It's as if the town is repeating one of my mother's refrains, 'Life is tedious', but without her dry ironical expression.

Anthony shifted in his seat and made to open the car door. 'But yeah, I'm sorry you didn't come from an ancient hill-top village as well,' he said.

He didn't really care, but he had the usual escapist fantasies; it would have been nice to be walking from the family's vineyard down cobbled streets to sit in a shady square drinking pastis and afterwards doing some research in the local medieval church. He could handle that. So could I.

★

It wasn't all talk. Anthony and I had left Australia together only a few years before, after our sons had grown and before we moved to the city. Because we had become parents at the beginning of our twenties we hadn't traipsed across Asia and around Europe like many of our newly footloose generation. It was decades later, at the beginning of the new millennium, before we flew across the mountains and plains with our plan of living in Paris for a year. I'd pressed my nose to the aeroplane window, trying to see the family farm below. It wasn't an altogether unreasonable aim: our farm was under the Sydney to Darwin to Europe flight path and all through my childhood my brothers and sisters and I watched the jet planes fly high overhead, making narrow white trails across the sky on their way to the rest of the world, our hearts filling with longing.

There below me were the memory-ghosts of the brother who became an artist, and the one who ended up a blokey Buddhist, and the youngest one who played in the Aboriginal cricket team, and the schoolteacher who preferred to fly and the one who married an Aborigine, and the older sister who became a nurse, and the little sister who sat drifting on the back step half the day; all of us eight kids standing on our patch of ancient ground, dreaming of somewhere else.

It felt melancholic to be looking down at the square drought-brown paddocks. Twenty-five years later and yet another long cycle of drought. The farm was definitely somewhere beneath me, but I had to acknowledge that 47,000 feet was too far above the ground to recognise any landmarks with certainty.

There is something about flying that creates detachment in me – an eternal now, the past never was and there never will be anything else. It's as if being in the God position – looking down – creates the exact image for being able to see myself. I didn't much like what I saw as I flew out over the edge of Australia. Someone, someday soon, would find out that I wasn't who I said I was. Not that they would discover I was someone else, but they would see how carefully I had made myself, a pastiche of thoughts, desires, memories to ward off dissolution.

I remembered a dream I had one night when I was no more than five or six years old. In the dream, there was a large airy spinning object like a Catherine wheel, which I somehow knew was the entire universe, and a tiny spinning shape, which I knew to be myself. The large Catherine wheel shape tried to absorb me and I knew that if it did, I would no longer exist. I struggled with all my might and with pure terror. Just as the large spinning shape was about to succeed, I awoke, petrified. I was comforted by my mother and went on through the remaining years of country childhood as solid as the earth beneath my feet. If occasionally the feeling of insubstantiality floated back, I ignored it.

I persuaded myself that was just the state of transition making me feel unanchored. I was a traveller to the centre of the imaginary world. I came from the far reaches of Western civilisation and I was heading for its heart. I was an innocent and curious man, tallish and thin, wearing a narrow coat to my ankles and carrying some kind of duffle bag. I was the Striding Man, a mythic figure. My face was a little weatherworn, I wasn't young, but still as eager as a youth, and I walked with easy strides. I was travelling towards the great city I had only heard about from other travellers' tales.

The Striding Man felt clear inside me, like an ancestor. Not one of the wild Irish Reidys and Kennedys who, my mother said, lay drunk around the bottom of Ponto Hill, or the hard-working English Whitehouses, but Pieter Josef Müller who, our branch of the family says, came from south-western Alsace, the part that was snatched back and forth between Germany and France. According to family lore, he was born in a village there in 1836, which, if true, actually makes him French, overturning years of family history. Either way, some years later he made his way to a seaport and then to Sydney, Australia and eventually to Wellington.

It was only fancy. Who did I think I was, swanning off to Paris? All the Millers – Müller became Miller, legend had it, around the First World War – were sturdy, short, peasant-looking folk who would have trudged steadily rather than strode elegantly, coat flying. You couldn't accuse any of them of being dreamy, romantic travellers. Pieter Müller arrived in Wellington in the 1850s and his descendants have been there tilling the soil ever since.

One hundred and fifty years later, his great, great, great granddaughter flew over the family farm, across the coast of Australia, halfway around the planet to finally circle over the Ile de France and Paris, her mind drugged with anticipation. The Imagined Life was taking physical form, and I was deeply puzzled. Despite believing in it for so long, my brain could not quite grasp how those pictures stored in imagination could exist outside it. As the flight descended, my mind, slightly unhinged by tiredness and jetlag, shuttled back and forth across its constructions, a blind weaver in the dark. The bright world of childhood memory seemed no more than a film I had once seen.

From the oval jet window, I joyfully recognised the patch-work of summer cultivation below: squares of yellow wheat fields, lemon-green meadows, cut-outs of dark green fairytale forest, stone villages, church spires, a chateau. I felt a pang of longing.

'Is it real?' I asked.

'It's as real as you need it to be,' Anthony said.

Months later when I felt I might belong there in Paris, I saw paintings of Montmartre when it was still a wooded hill dot-ted with vineyards and windmills and of the Seine when the gardens of grand houses swept down to its edge, and desper-ately wished it was my place, my history, my ancestors who said and did and thought this place into being. How quickly and easily I found myself unfaithful. There was no conflict, just an easy slipping into the arms of the Imagined World. I wondered how the connection to the land of my childhood, those few square miles of Wiradjuri country, could be thrown off so lightly.

6

Keeping Out of Trouble

My mother, 'pretty Connie Whitehouse' as my father, the most romantic of the solid Millers, used to call her, was waiting for us on the veranda of her retirement unit. It was only a one-room unit, poky compared to the sprawling house she'd had to sell after the stroke. She was sitting on the cane chair my sister had bought her, ready for someone to talk to, a woman in her late eighties who had lived her life within a small sphere. She had been born in Wellington to John Whitehouse, house-painter and trumpet player, and Linda Reidy, barmaid, in a little house only a few streets away. Half a kilometre or so wasn't a long way to go in more than eighty years, but she did travel in her mind, being a great reader despite refusing to go back to school after she had rheumatic fever when she was twelve years old.

We gave her the fruit and biscuits we had bought at the ugly Bi-Lo supermarket, a bit shame-faced because my mother had doggedly refused to shop there herself when she could still walk down the street. She wasn't going to support a supermarket that would put people she knew out of business. But since then the family grocery store belonging to my eldest brother's friend had closed, so there was no point in holding out any longer. And anyway, as everyone said, the supermarket did give young people jobs and kept them out of trouble.

Keeping out of trouble has not been that easy in Wellington. I had found out in my post-dream reading that, apart from the Native Title claim, Wellington had made the national newspapers for only two reasons over the last two decades. One was a murder down the road from our farm: 'I shot lotto winner's standover man, honest,'; the other was the overall crime rate. Crime was always one of the main topics of conversation with shopkeepers and with my mother's friends, most of who had had their houses broken into at least once.

My mother was mugged a few years ago. She was in her seventies then and still living in her own house. She was walking home over the railway bridge when she noticed some children watching her. The older ones were about ten, a younger one perhaps six, the Artful Dodger, as Mum called him. My mother was alert because Dorothy, her older sister, had been mugged on the same route home a few months before. A girl had ridden past, grabbed her bag and knocked her to the ground. Dot, being a feisty character, had clambered up and given chase for a block or two despite her bleeding shin, but there's not a lot a feisty woman in her late seventies can do, so she had to admit defeat and reported the incident to police.

As she came off the bridge, my mother thought the children had disappeared, although as she crossed Simpson Street she saw the Artful Dodger standing on the other side of the road. A minute later the boy ran past, lifting her bag and frightening her but not knocking her down, before tearing up the street ahead of her.

'He did it so well, his teacher would have been proud,' she said dryly.

She made a half-hearted attempt at giving chase but she had no chance of keeping up with the kids. She reported the theft to police who questioned people in the street and found her bag, minus about $40 cash, under the veranda of an empty house. As with Dorothy's assailants, the police had a good idea about the identity of the thieves, a group of Aboriginal kids. The thing was, both Dorothy and my mother refused to 'notice' whether the children were Aboriginal or not.

Years later, Mum still said, 'Everyone asked, were they Aboriginal? And no-one asked, were they white? Even people you wouldn't expect to ask.' When I pressed her recently, she reluctantly allowed that they might have been Aboriginal kids with a trailing-off tone that implied it was none of my business if they were.

Around the muggings period, my son's Christmas present bike was stolen from my mother's backyard, and twice, after my father died, her house was broken into. The second time, her engagement ring was stolen. The police identified 'persons of interest', but no-one was ever charged for any of these thefts, muggings or break-ins. I don't know if the 'persons of interest' were Aboriginal; my mother never offered any opinion, nor asked the police the race of anyone involved.

Other people in Wellington were not so discreet. According to the stories I've heard every time I return to Wellington, the response is simple and without variety: Aborigines commit

most of the crimes and the crimes only diminish when a particular group is in jail for a year or two.

'Abos,' they say, 'Abos.' With a particular note of contempt
in their voices.

I've never known what to say when this term, this tone, is
used. They are people I have known all my life.

At least no-one says boong or coon anymore.

I sat down beside my mother. 'How's it going?' I said.

'Not too bad,' she said. 'But life can be tedious, can't it?'

She said it dryly, not bitterly, but it still disturbed me. Her
eyesight had faded so much that reading and cryptic crosswords were slipping inexorably out of reach and lately the
nurses had started to help her dress, but my mother wasn't
allowed to be tired of life. Her body was slumped as if the
effort of coming out onto the veranda to greet us had been
too much. She had left her walking frame inside the unit, trying to pretend as long as she could that she didn't really need
it. I fingered the book I had brought up for her. We sat and
watched galahs squabbling around the birdbath in the garden.

'Poor Ruth Richardson,' said my mother.

I looked over and saw Mrs Richardson walking carefully
along the veranda. She had lived on one of the farms in Suntop near us and had always dressed smartly and had a 'proper'
house, not like our messy falling-down place with a fibro
'lavvy' out the back. Her house was painted white and had
wide verandas and a green lawn and roses in the garden.

'Why?' I said. 'What's the matter with her? She's not living
here now, is she?'

'No. She's just staying for a couple of weeks. She's going back home. She's been very brave about it. She's a lovely woman.'

'Brave about what?'

'A young Aborigine broke into her house, he was only nineteen, they said, and he attacked her. Ruth has been very brave but she was shattered.'

My mother had named him as Aboriginal. She had never done that before. It must be even worse than it sounded. I watched Ruth stop, straighten resolutely and knock on some-one's door further along the veranda. Her hair was softly waved, her summer skirt and blouse in matching soft blues, the kind of well-made appearance I have never known how to create.

'Was he from Wellington?'

'I don't know. I think so.'

'Was she raped?' It seemed a stupid question, Ruth was in her eighties, as old as my mother.

My mother nodded.

We didn't say anything else, but I could feel my skin burn-ing. I didn't want to think about it. It seemed an invasion of Ruth's privacy to even know about it. My mother had always been so disciplined about not gossiping. How could anyone go about his or her ordinary daily business in a town where such a thing had happened?

When we returned to Sydney I checked the crime figures for Wellington on the Bureau of Crime Statistics website. It surely couldn't be as bad as a few horrible stories made it sound.

It was worse.

For a range of crimes, including sexual assault, domestic violence, break-and-enter, weapons offences and malicious damage, Wellington was consistently from 150 to 300 per cent higher than the state average. Although the bureau didn't offer a statistical breakdown of offenders by Aboriginality, it did supply a breakdown of persons of interest by Aboriginality for each category of crime. A 'person of interest' is someone suspected or accused of committing a crime. Almost every crime – everything except fraud – registered far higher numbers of Aboriginal than non-Aboriginal persons of interest.

Wellington has a larger proportion of Aboriginal residents than most country towns because of 'the Mission' at Nanima, an Aboriginal settlement just outside of town, a remnant of the system of Aboriginal reserves set up more than a hundred years ago. I was curious about it as a child, but had never been there. No-one I knew had ever been there. It was only a few kilometres outside town but it was out of sight, hidden on the other side of the hills surrounding the Wellington Valley. By the 1960s, most Aborigines were living in town although dozens of families still lived at Nanima.

I looked for more statistics. Crime was not the only problem for Aborigines: the rates of diabetes, cardiovascular disease, hospitalisation for alcohol-related health problems and for youth victims of violence were all hundreds of per cent higher than in the white population. Still, despite every disadvantage, the Aboriginal population in Wellington was growing. At the turn of the millennium, it numbered 1075, about a quarter of the total population. More people were admitting to Aboriginality, but the birth rate was higher than in the white population as well. In fact, the white population graph for the central west looked like a spindly tree, thin at the youthful bottom with a wide, elderly, out-of-balance branch at the top, while the Indigenous graph was a pyramid, wide at the youthful bottom and tapering to old age at the top. The pyramid looked more solid, more lasting, than the tree.

But the negative figures continued: the rate of Aboriginal students finishing school was three times lower than the general population; the majority of Aboriginal children lived in one-parent families; an incredible fifty-four per cent were not in the paid work.

There was nothing new in any of this. It's the twenty-first century, more than 200 years after the invasion, but when you lose a war, you probably don't expect to be still suffering two centuries later. At the same time, I didn't know if any of these facts and figures truthfully revealed why my aunt and mother, both of them poor all their lives, were mugged in their seventies. Or why, in my innocent-looking town of rose gardens and Federation homes, Mrs Richardson was raped at eighty-two years of age.

7

Memory and Place

Rose wasn't answering my calls. My only other lead was a piece of paper with 'Gaynor Macdonald, Sydney Uni', written on it. Apparently she taught anthropology and had researched Wiradjuri culture. Before I rang her, I heard a crow calling mournfully outside the window, a sound I used to be able to reproduce perfectly. As kids, we spent hours practising imitations of bird calls: magpies, kookaburras, plovers, crows. That long slow *aaarrrk, aaarrrk, aaawwww* was my speciality. The crow cried outside in Kings Cross and reverberations of childhood suddenly multiplied all around me: the slope of the land beyond the wheat shed, the kurrajong tree by the gate, the exact lean of the gums down by the dry creek, the hide-smoothed rails of the cow yard, the corrugated iron shearing shed and the smell of sheep poo and wool, the bark of kelpie dogs, the pathetic bleating of sheep in the distance, the longing for rain that never came. There's the dust under my foot as I make pretend snake trails; there's the wood heap where the boys had to chop wood for the stove and where chooks' heads were cut off; there's the ramshackle chook yard with crows perched on the post on the lookout for an egg to snatch.

Crows were evil incarnate, not because they stole eggs but because they pecked the eyes out of ewes when they were giving birth and then plunged their cruel beaks into the newborn lambs. I had seen the hollow bleeding eye sockets of a still-living ewe and the entrails of the baby lambs torn out and left half eaten on the dirt before something had disturbed the crows' macabre feast. Sometimes, high above was an eaglehawk, waiting for its moment to descend and steal its share of the feast, but somehow I didn't extend my horror and condemnation to the eaglehawks. They always seemed more distant, less involved, not part of what happened on the ground. They were birds of the high places; we saw them circling around Baron Rock, gliding on currents of air, aloof from ordinary daily life.

I rang Gaynor. A soft, English-sounding voice answered and I felt curiously reassured.

'I was wondering if you can tell me anything about the Wiradjuri Native Title claim that was resolved a couple of weeks ago.'

'It wasn't a Native Title resolution.'

She explained that although the process had started as a Native Title claim, in the end it had not been a Native Title decision but a freehold grant under the Aboriginal Land Rights Act. Native Title is simply the recognition of pre-existing rights based on traditional laws and an ongoing connection to the land. It does not give the rights of ownership, such as the right to sell it, but it does give the right to negotiate about what happens on that land. Land Rights grants, on the other hand, give freehold title or a perpetual lease.

Native Title came out of the Mabo decision in 1992 when the High Court ruled that Indigenous people had a legal title to their land based on their connections to it. It overthrew the false doctrine of *terra nullius*, which means not the doctrine of uninhabited land as I had thought, but 'unowned' land. It was the result of a case brought by Eddie Koiki Mabo, who had been stunned to learn that the land where he was born, Mir Island off the north coast of Australia, which he had always thought he and his family owned, was in fact owned by the Crown. He died before the case was resolved, but the name of a small, dark-skinned man with a halo of hair became the name of the case that restored the original Australians' title to the land they had lived on for 40,000 years.

'But the first post-Mabo claim was made in Wellington?' I was scrambling, trying to show I did know something.

'Yes. I was the consulting anthropologist on the claim for several years.'

'Oh. Okay. So you know Rose Chown?'

'Yes. But I haven't had much to do with her for a while.'

'I've rung her, but so far she won't talk to me.'

'She can be elusive. Have you tried Joyce Williams?'

So Joyce *was* involved.

Gaynor went on to warn there might be problems if I talked to both Joyce and Rose. They were on opposite sides. On one side was the Wiradjuri Wellington Aboriginal Town Common Committee; Rose Chown was the spokesperson and the centre of media attention. On the other side were the Nanima Progress Association and the Wellington Aboriginal Corporation, meaning Bill Riley and Joyce and the Carrs and Stanleys, along with several other families.

So that was what the sudden coolness in the conversation with Rose was all about. I had wrecked my chance because I hadn't known what was going on. I didn't even know exactly where The Common, the land they were arguing over, was. I had an idea it was out along the Macquarie River somewhere, but it was floating in my mind, not located anywhere exactly.

I thought about our farm, Marylands. It was precisely anchored, had exactness; I could follow the road out past the showground and through the hills to Fingerpost and down along Anderson's creek and then up past the abandoned school and the first right past the tin church. I could see the old wooden farmhouse by the dry creek at the end of a bumpy lane. I could have walked along the lane blindfolded and not stumbled.

I remember dreamily walking along the new lane from the gate to the farmhouse. The old lane was in the flat paddock along the creek, but it was boggy and sometimes impassable when it rained, so my father made a new road using a blade attached to the front of the blue tractor. I can still remember the first lane, but it has the feel of myth now, the pearly sheen of indistinctness, whereas the second lane is shiny bright. It is sandy and gravelly underfoot; there is lucerne and wheat growing on the side; there are flies buzzing at my back; there is a blood knee where I fell on the gravel; there are squabbles with brothers and younger sister; there are cattle looming and staring in their impenetrable way; there are lambs who run

after us thinking we are their mothers, making us feel special
that a creature has chosen us.

I am not really dreaming; in fact, I am concentrating deeply
as I am composing a poem. It is early morning and I am walking the kilometre to the farm gate where we will climb into
the back of the teacher's ute and be driven the rest of the way
to school. The paddock has been planted with spring wheat,
which is now about ten centimetres high; delicate blades of
new wheat, on this morning sparkling with millions of dew
diamonds, each one splitting the light into red and blue and
emerald green fire. The beauty moves me deeply; in fact, I
don't think I have ever seen anything so beautiful in my entire
life. I feel the ache of desire to capture and convey the beauty.
I don't know if I have ever had that ache before. I see the dew
prisms splitting the sunlight, I see the rhythmic rows of wheat
serried up the slope, the bright freshness of the shoots, and I
shift and slide words in my brain. Stars, diamonds, glittering
wand, twinkle, sparkle. I come up with a bouncy, rhyming
poem that will stay in my head for the rest of my life like a
banal pop song.

Another year and later in the season, when the wheat is
nearly over our heads, my little sister and I find a secret 'room',
a clear space in the paddock where the soil is too sandy to
allow any wheat to grow. In there, just away from the lane,
we cannot be seen, or think we can't be. Like a pair of large
bowerbirds, we decorate the sandy floor of our room with
coloured bits of broken plates, flowers, buttons, old costume
jewellery and then we lie down and gaze at the clouds, telling
each other what shapes we can see.

In the top corner of this paddock, over the hill and well out

of sight of the house, is a stand of tired-looking pines where I
have my famous English picnic. Deep in Enid Blyton fantasy,
I persuade my younger brother and sister to have a picnic just
like children in a book. Despite my best efforts, the dried
peanut butter sandwiches arranged on a tea-towel spread on
the sheep poo under the spindly pines do not convince. The
desolate heat and scratchy Paterson's curse overrule my story.
That failure too stays with me for the rest of my life.

The constructed world dominated even out in the central west, hundreds of miles from the city. Roads, paddocks,
crops, sheds, English trees unhappily growing outside their
own soil. There wasn't much of the uncultivated world of the
Wiradjuri left by the time several generations had ploughed
and harrowed and sown and harvested.

Some of my memories do attach to the actual soil though,
and the native trees, and the creek, which must have been
there when the Wiradjuri wandered by with their axes, a
shallower channel before the land had been cleared and flood
waters rushed down slopes into the gully, but essentially
the same. The creek was dry nearly all the time, only flowing after a good storm or long steady rain. We stood on the
veranda and listened to the glorious roar of water and watched
the brown tumult for a couple of hours until it all disappeared
again. Then we went down and inspected the new headland
or island or peninsula carved out by the rush of water, or a
tree branch caught in the waterhole, or a sheep drowned.

I remember the different qualities of the ground beneath
my feet too: the warm summer dust outside the front gate, the
clay in the creek that the swallows used one year to make their
wonderful mud tunnels, the grains of sand on the ant mound

by the sheep yards, the clods of red earth in the ploughed pad-docks, the damp soil near the bottom waterhole. I remember the configuration of limbs on gum trees and kurrajongs: the one that split into two trunks where cattle used to rub their backs; the one with raised roots we could play cars in; the one my brother carved a large face into which was ever after known as the ghost tree. I remember the sky: endlessly blue for too long; the trail of a jet making a narrow road in the sky; the extraordinary whorl of a freak tornado that arrived one day and tore the huge pepper tree next to the house right out of the ground; the vermilion sunsets behind Baron Rock caused by volcanic eruptions in Indonesia in the 1960s; the thrilling build of thick puffy cumulus clouds and the peaceful drumming of rain on the roof.

8

The Common and Nanima Reserve

I spent the next several weeks at home researching. First, I located the Common. It was to the east of town, the opposite side to our farm, 183 hectares of gentle grassy hills stretching from the outskirts of Wellington on the south-eastern side to the Macquarie River as it bends back around to Nanima Reserve. Nanima is a separate parcel of about forty hectares, bordered on one side by the river and not subject to claim. The Town Common was first established by the Town Common Committee in 1867, marking the official moment the land was taken from the Wiradjuri. For quite some time I thought that theft was nothing to do with me.

I hadn't known anything about the Common as a child, but even out on the farm, I'd heard about Nanima. I knew that was where most of the Aborigines lived and didn't question why they had a separate village. I didn't actually go there until my early twenties when I was doing a university assignment on 'race relations in a country town'. I drove around interviewing whites and Aborigines with my chunky late-seventies tape recorder, feeling very sophisticated. It's more than twenty-five years ago now and the details are hazy in my mind, but I remember taking the road out to Nanima as if I was on a trek into unknown Africa. The landscape seemed different, unfamiliar. Dry spiky grass, strange rocks, disturbing gullies. I drove over a hill then came into a small settlement of neat fibro houses with wire fences. I don't recall any gardens.

The impression left after almost three decades is of bareness, of houses stuck on a landscape rather than settled into it. No-one would really talk to me except the white schoolteacher. I did try to interview a bunch of Aboriginal women but they laughed a lot and refused to speak into the tape recorder.

I had not been back there since. Even when I was earnestly doing my race relations research, I had not thought to find out anything about the history of Nanima, but although it wasn't part of the claim, it was the reason that so many Wiradjuri and other Aborigines were living on the Common. It was originally part of a network of Crown land specifically 'reserved' for Aboriginal use. The more I read about the system of reserves the more it started to look as if, inadvertently, it might have 'set-up' the opposing sides of the title fight a century later.

Reserves were created because, in the fifty or so years after the first white settlement, there had been bloody guerrilla warfare between the white invaders and black defenders – not that the legislators would have described them in those terms. It was decided to allow Aborigines their own land for 'secure' occupation in the hope of reducing the conflict. The British

House of Commons stated in the 1830s that the Aborigines had 'a plain right and a sacred right' to their land but it was, in a sense, managing prisoners of war.

In the 1880s, a Protector of Aborigines was appointed and the Aboriginal Protection Board created to manage reserves. It was recommended that reserves be established away from towns so that 'the corrupting influence of Europeans was limited', a noble-sounding segregation. At the same time as separating Aborigines from Europeans, all Aborigines were treated as one people, tribal identity was disregarded altogether. Often, people from different and possibly warring tribes were forced to live on one reserve.

A report from 1915 by the Aboriginal Protection Board states:

Nanima, Wellington: The schoolroom presents a cheerful appearance, and everything about it is kept clean and tidy. Reading and recitation are both creditable. Suitable poetry is memorised. Writing uniformly good. In arithmetic problems are freely used, and the work is generally accurate. In drawing, needlework, and singing, good work is done. Manual work includes paper folding, netting, and raffia work, and is a source of general interest.

It sounds so pleasant, so resolutely civilised. This was what I believed about life at Nanima when I was a child; that life was a round of reading, arithmetic, drawing, needlework, singing, raffia work. Why shouldn't everyone live happily ever after?

Naturally, that's not the way it was. Aboriginal people had to ask permission to leave the reserve, to get a job or even to get married. They could be – and were – moved from one reserve to another without being asked. They could not own a house or any land and their homes and mail could be searched without their permission. Their daily lives were regimented and the smallest of transgressions could result in severe punishments. There was also a complete ban on any traditional Indigenous celebrations and on their language and customs. On many reserves, even their names had to be Anglicised. Many children were taken away from the supposed 'bad influence' of their families. Some parents were forced to leave their children by the threat of having their rations cut.

It didn't end in the nineteenth century. Until I was a teenager, Aborigines could only vote in some states; they were not counted in the general census; they did not have freedom of movement. If they had a 'preponderance of Aboriginal blood' – or if they lived on a reserve, no matter what their percentage of Aboriginal blood – they could not receive old age, invalid or widow's pensions, nor any maternity allowance. They could, however, apply for a Certificate of Exemption, which meant they would not be legally considered to be Aboriginal, their identity erased. In effect, it certified you were not who you were born as! If you signed it and had a character reference from a 'respectable' white person such as a teacher or policeman, you were exempt from the laws that controlled the lives of the rest of your people. You had a new identity – although it could be revoked if any of its conditions were broken. These certificates were in force until the referendum of 1967 that allowed Aborigines to be counted as citizens. It was the year I started high school in Wellington.

I try to imagine complete powerlessness in my own country,

the humiliation of having others direct my life: my sons being taken away from me; the impossible-to-heal tearing of the heart; the erasure of everything that tells me who I am – kinship, country, language. No bloody wonder, I thought, no bloody wonder the domestic violence, the alcohol, the drugs, the sexual violence, the break-ins, the street muggings. No bloody wonder at all.

I thought about Mrs Richardson at home in her own house, never feeling safe again. None of it was her fault but she had been cruelly made to pay for it.

9

In Search of an Inland Sea

I tried to ring Rose again. It was January by now, the middle of a long hot spell. My red hair and freckled face, made for the Irish coolness of my mother's ancestors, felt damp and sticky and my determination seemed to melt as well. It was difficult to make the effort to ring someone who probably didn't want to talk to me. I just wanted to lie on cool lino in front of a fan with a wet flannel on my face. On the fifth attempt of the week, Rose finally answered.

'You're a hard woman to get hold of.'

'Yeah, I'm outside most of the time. Trees I planted need waterin' in this heat.'

'God, that'd be hard work. Do you have a hose, or buckets?'

'Buckets. Got a tap an' buckets.' Her voice was matter-of-fact, a dark-brown depth to it, like earth, but held back as well.

I realised she was not going to talk to me. There was a tone of regret in the ordinary things she was saying, as if she didn't want to hurt my feelings.

'I've decided to get on with writing my own book instead,' she said. She had given it serious thought and was sorry to let me down but she was firm.

'That's good,' I said, my heart banging in disappointment. 'It's good to write your own book.' And then rapidly, 'But I'd like to try to explain what I want to do. I didn't really make it clear before. I come from Wellington, from Wiradjuri land, but I've lost my connection to it. I thought writing about it might help me. I don't mean to take your story, but just to find my connection to it.'

I nervously reiterated and wandered and corrected myself, but I must have said something useful.

'I'll take your telephone number,' she said eventually. 'I might give you a ring myself some time.'

Some chance! It had taken long enough to get hold of her when I had the power to ring her; it would be as good as never if she were supposed to be ringing me. But it was all that was on offer so I slowly and clearly repeated my number.

'I really would love to meet you,' I said.

When I put the receiver down, tears sprang. With a bit more effort I could find others to talk to, but my first step was now a gaping hole.

I couldn't give up on Rose yet. I went to the study and wrote a long letter explaining my desire to find the story of my place. I wrote the letter quickly, rushed up to the post office and posted it. It seemed strange, something from another century, to write a pleading letter, put it an envelope, stick a stamp on it and drop it in the postbox. Surely such a simple way of sending messages should work.

★

Years ago, Bill Riley had told me that his people believed the willy wagtail was a messenger. He said it would bring messages from your family hundreds of miles away.

'We didn't need phones.' He grinned, his arms folded at my mother's table.

I scribbled notes, trying to hold his eye at the same time. It had taken me weeks to track him down. Mum brought us tea in her 'good' cups and fruit cake, and listened too. Bill seemed pleased to have a small audience and had extended his visit.

I nodded. Out on the farm under Baron Rock, we kids all thought the willy wagtail was telling us something. It always flew up in a tiny whir of black-and-white wings and fan-shaped tail and then darted and hopped about us, spreading its feathers and getting our attention while it chirruped something intently. One of my brothers – he became a teacher – stated that it said 'sweet pretty creature' but I thought it was saying something different every time.

Or perhaps, on the lookout for secret messages, I just hoped it was. Reading had given me the sense that there was a parallel world of adventure and beauty alongside the ordinary one, if only I could find a way through. Sometimes, when I was out walking, I would turn quickly, my shoulder forward, hoping to turn at just the right spot to slip sideways through the narrow door into the parallel world. I suppose it was a longing for something else to happen, for the ordinary to stretch its dusty skin and the extraordinary to burst through in all its glory.

Somewhere along the way out of childhood, the idea of the extraordinary was transmuted into the actual world beyond those paddocks and that town, especially the world of Europe. I suppose that was when the Striding Man was born. I longed for the world on the other side of the planet, a land floating on clouds in my head. The Imagined World. It grew and grew inside my brain, nourished by books and occasional films, until it took up all the space.

In anyone's reckoning, how could one-horse Wellington and a few Wiradjuri arguing about a mere 200 years of dusty recorded history acted out under gum trees compete with Paris and all her lights. Wellington had no Picasso, no Notre Dame or Pei pyramid, no Sartre, no Molière, no Victor Hugo. No revolutionary heroes, kings, courtesans, palaces. No corner bistros, no cobbled lanes, no balconies balanced above teeming streets, no dream of itself as the centre of the world.

Until the morning of my terse dream, the answer was always obvious. I didn't understand why it had changed, why suddenly the story of the place I came from might matter.

My ancestors lived in Wellington for five generations before me; their bones must be part of the soil by now, mixing with bones of Wiradjuri people and rotting trees and decomposing grasses. Some of my forebears may have killed Wiradjuri, one perhaps had children with them. My story mingled with the Wiradjuri story a long time ago. But how had my ancestors come to be there in the first place? What was anyone doing out there so far from civilisation? While no-one was talking to me, I started reading the explorers' journals and histories held at the Mitchell Library in Sydney.

Wellington's white history officially started when John Oxley was asked by Governor Lachlan Macquarie to explore the land west of Bathurst in 1817. This was only twenty-nine years after the first white settlement in Australia and no-one had any clue about the extent, let alone the geography, of the country they were in. Oxley's job was to find out whether the Lachlan and Macquarie rivers flowed into a huge inland sea as people generally supposed they must.

I've always liked the inland sea idea. It's so optimistic – a gigantic circle of scalloped beaches and palm trees in the middle of Australia with Uluru as a fantasy island in the middle. Sun glinting on waves, giant waterslides down the Rock, children splashing at the water's edge or building sandcastles, lovers walking hand in hand along the sand, teenagers eating fish and chips wrapped up in newspaper. There would be thousands of kilometres of resorts, shopping centres, high-rise apartments – casinos too, probably.

But all Oxley found at the end of the Macquarie was a swamp full of waterbirds. There were sacred kingfishers, ibis, egrets, cormorants, spoonbills and herons, as well as cockatiels, snipe, sandpipers and godwits, some of which, it has since been discovered, migrate from as far away as Siberia, China and Japan. This was all very well, but no substitute for an inland sea.

Along the way, however, at the junction of the Macquarie and Bell rivers – the present location of Wellington – Oxley found, on 19 August 1817, 'a second Vale of Tempe', the first being a valley in Thessaly in ancient Greece, celebrated for its 'beauty, cool shade and warbling birds'. He must have arrived in a good season because he went on to say, 'Imagination cannot fancy anything more beautifully picturesque than the scene which burst upon us.' He described the noble and magnificent reaches of the river full of fish and mussels, swans and ducks, the grassy flats replete with emus and kangaroos, the beautiful hills and open valleys of greatest possible fertility spreading in every direction.

According to his compass and calculations, the location was latitude 32.32.45 south and longitude 148.51.30 east. That must have been the first time anyone used a compass in my home town.

Oxley said it was clear that the Aborigines they met along the way had already heard about them and knew they had useful implements such as axes and knives, but there is no mention of seeing any Aborigines in the Wellington Valley during the few days they stayed there. The fact is, not only were the Wiradjuri already there, but also white stockmen. Oxley's diaries note evidence of herds of cattle at the river's edge and a campsite, but there's no official record of Europeans being there. History – indeed, time itself in European minds – began in Wellington the day John Oxley arrived and, although he didn't know it, the clank of chains and swish of the lash were soon to be added to the 'warble of birds' in the vale of Tempe. Wiradjuri country was about to become a large outdoor jail.

The new governor, Thomas Brisbane, liked the idea of 'the better sort of convict' being sent to country penal settlements rather than being kept in Sydney. He declared it would give them protection from shame, but it turns out that many of the 'better sort' of convict were political dissidents, likely to cause unrest, so it's not unreasonable to suspect he had other motives for sending the troublesome as far away as possible – and out of sight.

The site chosen was a few kilometres from the junction of

the Bell and Macquarie rivers, within the traditional camping ground of the local Wiradjuri. The man to set it up was young Lieutenant Percy Simpson, who arrived in Wellington in February 1823 with a group of thirty soldiers, fifty 'special' convicts, and some cows and sheep and wheat. And, heaven help her, his young wife, Hester McNeill.

Knowing how hot Wellington is in February, often above thirty-five degrees Celsius, and how many clothes women wore at that time – long dresses, stays, petticoats, pantaloons – it must have been near unbearable for Hester under the canvas tent. With all those felons about, I don't imagine she was able to go about bare-armed or bare-legged, let alone lie outside and ponder the vast velvet-black sky aglow with stars as we had on summer nights. In the mornings, hot by 9 o'clock, she would have bathed in a tin dish and put on her pantaloons and petticoats and thought about the Wiradjuri women with their magnificent oiled black skins swimming and splashing in the river. In the evenings she would have gratefully taken off most of the layers and lain sweating on the bed next to Lieutenant Percy.

And then when their first winter arrived, it rained for two solid months. It does get properly cold in Wellington; I remember bitter frosts and pendants of ice under the outside taps each winter. I hated getting up for school in the chilly bedroom because there was no heating and no hot shower and, as well, the dash across the frosty grass to the broken fibro toilet. We did have a wood fire in the kitchen, which my father lit first thing in the morning, and we stood around it warming hands and feet. But all the other rooms, especially the bathroom with its tin dish of water, were as cold as the huts in 1823. Still, for Hester and the rest, the cold and wet would have been more familiar and therefore not as trying as the flattening heat.

Early May, though, should have been crisp and sunny. At that time of year there is a clarity to the air, a coolness in the mornings. These are days when it is good to be alive. I remember even my solid quiet father's spirits would lift to exclamation. He loved May days, and even better, 'May days in June' as he called them. He would sit on a kerosene tin just outside the back door, his knees apart and his hands clasped between them, his felt hat tilted back, lifting his face to the sun, receiving benediction.

Perhaps someone in those early days, a soldier, or even a convict, might have looked around and thought, maybe this is not so bad after all. A row of public buildings was erected up from the river: a commandant's house, a brick office, a military barracks, a weatherboard jail house, fourteen bark huts, a storehouse that also housed a courtroom, flour mill and engineers' department, and a house for a Wesleyan missionary. It looked like things were happening. At its height, the penal colony had 250 people and was supplying enough wheat for its own needs with a surplus.

But neither the soldiers nor the convicts wanted to be stuck out there in the middle of the unending bush, surrounded by possibly murderous Natives. There were none of the pleasures of Sydney town, no pubs and no women except Native women and Hester. The convicts 'lost' flocks of sheep and cattle, wouldn't work, tried to spoil crops – wheat, tobacco, potatoes, onions – pilfered food, burnt wheat stacks, waylaid supply carts; and the soldiers plotted against Simpson, circulating rumours about his mental health. Many of the convicts deserted, probably in the direction of the lost cattle and sheep, perhaps with Wiradjuri women.

Simpson was instructed to have friendly relations with the Natives, who were to be given rewards of tomahawks, wheat and fish hooks if they caught straying cattle or runaway convicts. It seems a bizarre introduction to a 'work for pay' economy and to European morality. I don't know whether the Wiradjuri did act as bounty hunters or not, although some diarists noted the 'Natives' distress' at the convicts being whipped, so perhaps they were not inclined to hand over runaways. I wondered what the Wiradjuri thought of these men who tied up their own tribesmen and flogged them until their backs ran with blood.

The penal settlement is just a paddock now on the eastern side of town, empty except for two signs, one saying *Site of First Convict Settlement, 1823–1831* and the other *Maynggu Ganai Site*, Wiradjuri for 'People's Land'. I've driven past it many times, not really taking much notice. An archaeological survey has identified the foundations of military barracks and mud huts, a dump of bricks on the Government House site and a few horseshoes and chains. That's all.

It was nearly autumn by now, but still hot. I sat in the Mitchell Library at a large desk covered with books and request notes and looked around at other researchers. Each was surrounded with similar paraphernalia, the luggage for a journey into the past. A few had left their outspread notes and books on their desks and stood at the open drawers of the old-fashioned index where cards had been painstakingly written in ink. They were mostly young university students, researching for history degrees, I imagined, and a few people like me on an obscure personal mission. Perhaps they too felt an uncertainty in their souls; perhaps it was a national malady. At the same time I had to acknowledge that I'd felt less amorphous in the months since the dream instruction than I had for several years. There was something in uncovering the story of Wiradjuri and Wellington that had almost immediately begun to soothe the gnawing uncertainty. It felt like a balm, quieting the restlessness, but it also felt as if there were nothing else I should be doing. It's a rare enough sensation for me, so rare that the only other times I have felt it have been when I gave birth to each of my sons and took care of them. It's the feeling of doing something that is not necessarily pleasurable or joyful, though it can be intensely so, but is unarguably necessary. Finding food for your family or jumping out of the way of a falling tree, such actions do not need to be considered or argued and there is an exquisite simple relief in action that is outside argument. I didn't know how the story of my one-horse town fell into that company, but it had, slipping in soundlessly like a loose page accidentally falling into the right place.

10

Who Will Talk to Me?

Rose still hadn't responded to my pleading letter. I didn't really think she would. I couldn't do anything more without seeming to harass her. Looking for more clues, I rifled through a box on the bottom shelf of my bookcase. The box contained notes and cards and photographs from workshops I had done with people in country towns writing their own lives. I found a snapshot of the Wellington Aboriginal Health Centre group. There was Joyce, small and neat and dainty. I turned it over and could not believe my luck. I had written her phone number on the back.

'Yes, I remember you,' Joyce said when I rang. 'Still got your book 'ere somewhere. Haven't seen it for a while.'

'Haven't you? Have you written any of your story?'

'Nah. Too busy. I'm teachin' Aboriginal culture to the high school kids. And I'm looking after four grandkids most of the time.'

'That's not a bad effort.'

'Well, I am eighty-four.'

Her voice was dry and ironic like my mother's, but stronger and more direct. Her accent was flat, a bit scratchy to my ears. She sounded like someone who was used to speaking her mind.

'You're just about the same age as my mother. I don't think she would be up to chasing grandkids.' I could hear my own accents flattening out. 'She's at Maranartha.'

'Oh yeah? She like it?'

'Yes, they are very good to her there. But Joyce, why I rang, I was wondering if you might have time to talk to me about the Native Title claim. Gaynor said you knew about it.'

There, I had jumped in and there was no going back. If she knocked me back, there was nowhere else to go.

'Listen,' said Joyce, 'Rose's committee left out Traditional Families and listed people who weren't even Aboriginal. John Riley, my grandfather, was on the list, he was *white*.' Her tone was disgusted. 'And John Ah See, he was on it – his great grandmother on his father's side was Chinese. And on his mother's side, her grandmother, Annie Rare, she was a Maori. So we've put in our own claim, the fourteen Traditional Families they left out. We've got a solicitor and we're goin' to sort it.' She had barely taken breath.

I was taken aback. I didn't know what she was talking about. I didn't know any of the people she mentioned, although it sounded like Joyce thought Rose's mob were not legitimate Wiradjuri. It also sounded as if another Native Title claim had been made. I'd thought the whole thing was finished with the land grant to Rose's committee.

'Can I come and see you, Joyce? I'd like to talk to you some more about this. I still come up to Wellington every month to see my mother.' Then I added weakly, 'I've meant to come and see you but I thought you would have forgotten me.'

'Not that old,' she said.

'No, I didn't mean it like that. I guess I was a bit shy.'

'No, don't be shy. Come and see me. I live in Swift Street, coupla streets over from where your mum used to live.'

'Yes, I know – Swift Street. Can I make a time to meet you?'

I didn't notice until later that although, as far as I knew, Joyce had never met my mother, she knew where she lived.

'Nah, give me a ring when you're up here next. I'm gunna be away for a few weeks. Then I'll be around. Any time during the week except the mornin's. I'll be teachin' in the mornin's.'

I put the phone down feeling unreasonably exhilarated. I looked back at the photograph of Joyce, standing with the others. She was grinning cheekily. Yes, she would talk to me.

11

The Mind of a Thief

Each morning on the way to the Mitchell Library I walked down the steep steps to Wooloomooloo Bay, past the grey Navy ships at dock and the wharf where my ancestors, convict and free, had clambered down the gangway onto Australian soil for the first time. I liked that I lived so near, a minute's walk, from where they had first landed. Then I climbed up the steps on the other side, past the Art Gallery and through the Domain to the sandstone steps and columns of the library entrance. There was the mosaic map of Terra Australis on the floor and the lovely white marble staircase sweeping up to the exhibition rooms, and directly in front of me, the high doors leading into the library proper; all of it reassuring that whatever was kept in this solid, elegant vault must be important. It protected knowledge and history, but also, I realised, power.

The Wiradjuri didn't keep written records in the early nineteenth century so I was never going to find their version of what had happened in the Wellington Valley. How did they fill in their days, apart from finding enough food? What did they think about, talk about? What did they feel when the white invaders walked onto their land?

I had to return to the white explorers and note-takers. Oxley remarked that when he met them, the Wiradjuri already knew that light-skinned people from the sea had come to 'sit', as they called it, on Dharug and Eora land on the other side of the mountains. The missionaries who arrived soon after, as well as one John Henderson, an English traveller, all moonlighted as amateur ethnologists in the Wellington Valley in the 1820s. It seems to have been the fashionable hobby for educated Englishmen of the time. They recorded the appearance, personalities and practices of the Wiradjuri from their nineteenth-century English gentlemen's perspective. It's impossible to know how much to rely on them.

In one record, Tindale's Catalogue, I came across more than fifty English spellings of Wiradjuri:

Iradyuri, Wiradhuri, Wiraduri, Wiradjeri, Wirra' jerre', Wiradhari, Wirra-dhari, Wirradhurri, Wirra-dthoor-ree, Wirraidyuri, Wirraddury, Wiraijuri, Wirraijuri, Wi-iratheri, Wirrathuri, Wiradthuri, Wiradthery, Wirathere, Wiratheri, Wiragere, Wuradjeri, Wira-durei, Wira-shurri, Wirradgerry, Weradgerie, Woradgery, Waradgeri, Wiratu-rai, Wiradurei, Wirrajerry, Weorgery, Woradjera, Woorad-gery, Woora-juri, Woradjerg, Weerarthery [said to be Ka-milaroi name], Wirotheree, Wiratheri, Wooratheri, Wooratherie, Wiira-durei, Wirra-dthooree, Warradjerrie, Waradgery, Wayradgee, Wirrajeree, Wirradjery, Wir-ra' jer-ree, Wirrai-yarrai, Wirrach-arree, Wiradjwri, Warrai Durhai, Wirraidyuri.

I wanted to see what the Wiradjuri looked like, what they did, how they occupied themselves, but if there were so many ways for the note-takers to hear and spell just one word, their observations of daily life must have been equally open to interpretation. But the note-takers' records were all I could find.

According to the number of mussel shells and axes found, Wiradjuri camped around fires near the Bell River and along the Macquarie on the other side of present day Nanima for tens of thousands of years. Europeans brought smallpox, which swept through, killing many, but they still lived a traditional life when the missionaries arrived. In a clan group of about eighty, they fished for yellow bellies, cod, catfish, turtles and yabbies, and collected mussels and hunted duck, emu and kangaroos and dug up fat grubs and roots that tasted like chestnuts and roasted them in their fires to make a feast. They gathered quandong fruit and wattle gum and caught wild bees, attaching a piece of feather-down to their sticky feet then following them back to their hives to eat their sweet honeycomb.

I suddenly realised I had lived on this land for all my childhood and adolescence and had not eaten a single item of food that originally came from its soil or animals or rivers. My father grew wheat in lovely green rows that he harvested and drove down to the silo at the railhead where it was freighted to Sydney and sold to Australian flour mills and Chinese traders. He raised cattle and sheep too, which were trucked to the saleyards in Dubbo, the nearest large town. Once a week he killed a sheep, slitting its throat quickly and hanging it up under a gum tree overnight before carving it into cuts the next morning for his family to eat. I learned about Aboriginal children eating kangaroos and goannas in Social Studies lessons in our little one-roomed schoolhouse, but didn't think of such animals as food that ordinary people could eat. Now there is kangaroo steak in Woolworths in Kings Cross for the international backpackers, but it is still an oddity among the displays of beef and lamb.

The Wiradjuri received many visitors from other areas, clusters of young men or families, often daily, but it's impossible to tell if this was usual before the note-takers came, or whether the visitors were coming out of curiosity about the new pale-skinned arrivals. One day, as noted by one of the missionaries, the group of visitors was much larger – about thirty young men walked out of the bush at once. They were well built and tall, many of them over six feet.

A painting by Darwin's artist from the *Beagle* voyage, Earle Augustus, titled 'A Native of the Wellington Valley, 1826' shows a tall, muscular young man, his chest and upper arms intricately marked, not with tattoos, but the flesh itself carved. His hair, long and curly, is lifted away from his face by a headband and the long curls are separated like ringlets, rather than bushy. The ringlets, I read later, were due to the fish oil that Wiradjuri men and women rubbed into their hair. As I gazed at the image of the nameless young man, I realised he was about the same age as one of my sons. I wondered at the strange fate of becoming an ethnographic exhibit. I cannot even imagine such a thing happening to me, or anyone I know.

The group of visitors the missionary described was entirely naked, but others describe men wearing a net-like band of kangaroo tendon around their waists with a small tassel attached in front and behind; yet another records men wearing girdles of 'opossum' skin and 'opossum' skin cloaks neatly sewn with tendons. This particular group had decorated their faces and bodies with red and yellow ochre and white clay and had feathers in their hair. They were well armed, carrying fire-hardened spears over three metres long, a type of cudgel known as a nulla-nulla, a large war boomerang that the Wiradjuri called a bargan, and a narrow wooden shield, having obviously arrived to do battle.

I read that the night before battles, which were apparently often to do with territorial disputes, there was always a corroboree. The men painted their bodies with lines and shapes and added yellow plumes from white cockatoos' crests to their woven kangaroo tendon headbands, which Henderson, one of the note-takers, thought made them look as if they were wearing coronets. When evening came, he said, fires were lit and wild and noisy dancing began, enacting mock-battles, 'skirmishing with great order and exactness', or mimicking kangaroos, emus, goannas, the dancers slightly bending their knees and quivering their legs in time to the music.

It sounded like performances by Aboriginal dancers I've often seen at the openings of cultural festivals. Mid afternoon on an outdoor stage or in a local hall, after a speech or two by local notables, men and boys with white-painted bodies and wearing red loincloths dance in front of a mostly white audience. The dancers are always rhythmic, the sound of the didgeridoo is always deep and stirring, but there is no trace of the 'powerful excitement' that Henderson described. I can barely imagine what it would be like to see a corroboree where there was no sense of performance, only immersion in the ritual. The energy must have been nearly hallucinatory.

The women were at corroborees as well, seated to one side, and making music by beating on skins stretched between their knees, clacking small weapons together and singing. Henderson, who had recently arrived from India, said that the tunes were the same as those he had heard in Hindustan. He also likened some of the songs to ones he had heard in 'Bootan'. He made a number of parallels between the Wiradjuri and Indian tribal people, which, he said, indicated their common origins. He also gave a wildly romantic description of the general scene: 'The night was dark and cloudy; while the broad flame which illuminated the forest, threw a lurid and flickering glare upon their strangely distorted figures; the magic interest was likewise increased by the reflection, that these mimic representations were to be the prelude to a savage and deadly contest.'

As it turned out, he admits he was wrong about the savage battle because the dispute he mentioned was amicably settled by negotiation the next morning. It seems, most often, disputes were settled this way, by lively discussion between the warriors who argued not as a rabble but, according to Henderson, with the air of great speakers.

Henderson wrote too of local Wiradjuri spiritual beliefs. The original Creative Being was Baiame, one of whose sons was the evil Mudgegong, who changed most of Baiame's other children into animals. However, two, Melgong and Yandong (or Wandong) survived and were the progenitors

77

of the present-day Wiradjuri. Baiame is asleep now, but once woke up and rolled over, causing the sea to roll in. A few years later one of the missionaries, Günther, mentioned this same story in his diary:

> They speak of a very great flood, which a long time since covered the whole of this country, even hills & mountains. Many people were drowned, but a number were saved on an island, standing in a flat. They had houses there & the water kept aloof from them. Various other ridiculous tales are connected with it, such as, one man swimming about in the water for several months & kept alive, at last, it appears, he got into some cave & went under the ground for several miles, then coming out at a certain opening; not many miles off from here, which, they said, they would show me.

The missionaries didn't know about the series of caves near Wellington so I suppose the tale did sound ridiculous. I have been down into the caves and I also know that 'the flood-gates of the salt ocean were immediately thrown open and the hills and valleys disappeared beneath the rolling waters' as Henderson recorded, because as a child I had seen the evidence for myself. While I was still in primary school, I often explored the hills in the farm next to ours with my brothers and sister, hoping the rough, red-faced farmer who owned it wouldn't catch us tramping across his land. Our hearts beat nervously each time, but we were drawn on by the hope of discovery that seemed much more possible in his folded, bush-covered hills than in our bare, ploughed paddocks. His property had gullies and rocky outcrops and stands of gums and acacias and beckoning hilltops, while ours was only open country where nothing could be hidden.

One hot summer's day, all our daring was rewarded when we found fossils of shells and trilobites and sea-fronds in slabs of stone hidden in a gully. We had learnt about such things in our school lessons and knew they were important treasures. Sitting in the Mitchell Library years later, I remembered the utterly joyous thrill of discovery and could feel again the astonishment of a finding a seabed in the middle of the dry hills. The Wiradjuri must have seen fossils – and known what they meant. They knew the deep ocean had covered the land, and sea animals and weeds had floated down and become embedded in the mud and that Baiame had rolled over and the sea had slid off his body and he had become dry land again.

I was guiltily grateful, too, for Henderson's observations of the bora ground, a place of sacred ritual for the initiation of young men, one of the most important for all the Wiradjuri, located in a secluded part of the bush on the river bank. I didn't know where exactly but I hoped that Rose Chown or one of the other Wellington mob might be able to tell me. By coincidence, one of my brothers, Tim, was investigating its location at the same time. An artist, he had the quixotic desire to paint the landscape as it was before the Europeans arrived in Wellington. He said he'd been told the bora was on a property quite near the Native Title land, but he wasn't sure if it was true or not. I wanted to go there immediately to see if it would yield any of its past, but Tim wouldn't tell me its location until the property owner agreed to let him visit. He also reckoned we needed to talk with Joyce or, better, a Wiradjuri man, to find out if it was all right to see it.

The bora, according to Henderson, consisted of an avenue of eucalypt trees about a mile long, each tree carved with various symbols that represented humans transmogrified into animals – snakes, possums, emus, kangaroos – and other natural elements such as lightning and even meteors. At one end of this avenue was an earthen sculpture of a human figure lying on his breast and a representation of the eaglehawk's eyrie. Along the avenue, symbols of male and female reproductive organs were carved into the earth. There was also one carving, which to Henderson strongly resembled a lingam, the Hindu symbol of both the phallus and of the moment of creation – another piece of evidence in his argument on the origins of the Wiradjuri, but to me, evidence of a connection to my own past. I have an old cup on the window ledge in my study with lingam-shaped stones in it which I had collected for years, even before I had heard of the word. A lingam resembles a human cell as it begins to divide and for Hindus, it is the original shape, the beginning of duality, because it is the shape of one becoming two.

At the other end of the bora avenue, a narrow path to the left led to a circular clearing enclosed by an earthen wall. During initiation the young male was questioned by an elder disguised as an extraordinary being. If the youth was approved, he was led down the avenue by spear-wielding elders, stopping at each of the carvings as secret knowledge was conveyed, and finally led to the circle where he was seated on the wall. After the ceremonies he was sent out into the bush for a number of days during which he could see no-one. Once initiated, the young man was bound to obey strict laws, including a total avoidance of women until the elders said he was ready to marry.

Henderson asserts all this was explained to him by a man he refers to as a king of the tribe, who alone had the authority to reveal secrets. Even so, the 'king' said he would be killed – and perhaps the whole tribe killed – by neighbouring tribes if they knew he had revealed secrets to the uninitiated.

I feel uncertain about re-telling it myself, partly because I have no idea whether Henderson was reliable or not – perhaps he just made things up to make himself sound interesting – but more because I wonder if I am stepping too near what was secret knowledge. Still, both feelings are overruled by curiosity and the weary pragmatic thought that it doesn't matter any more – it's in Henderson's book for anyone to read.

And intriguing as they were, the ethnographic notes were not letting me get any closer to the daily life of the Wiradjuri. The events the note-takers had chosen to write about were not so much from daily life but rather what was spectacular, romantic, shocking. The actual way of life of the Wiradjuri, and their consciousness of being, still eluded me completely.

I've been avoiding writing about the women. Whatever I repeat from the note-takers, it will not look good. It appears that the women didn't participate in tribal meetings or discussions; that they were given at eleven or twelve years old to much older men who could bestow them as sexual partners on others if they wished; that they were buried sitting up, like men, but in unmarked graves, unlike the men, whose tribal origins were carved on a nearby tree. They did not mix with men in daily life, gathered food separately – grubs and fruits from the bush and mussels from the river – and they always sat at a different fire. It was observed that they were not permitted to eat meat until the men were finished and only if it was given to them. They were often described as very thin.

They must have had their own domains of power, women's business, their own lore of fertility and birthing and the gathering of food, and they must have taught their daughters stories of how to follow the honey-bee and what to do when the blood flowed from their bodies, but I have not been able to find records of any of this from the Wellington Valley. The records were made by white men, so of course they were not going to have access to female knowledge or practices.

But there were many reports of the women being beaten with weapons by their husbands. Too many accounts from too many sources to ignore. One eyewitness told of a high-status man in the Wellington Valley beating his wife with a boomerang, inflicting a wound to the bone. He also says the husband was sorry the next day and bathed her wound with warm water. Nothing new under the sun there.

My first reaction was to sit horrified with the missionaries, but the Wiradjuri had, I suppose, the same percentage of ill-tempered, violent husbands as in any other culture. No-one can see what happens each evening behind pretty gardens and charming verandas, but a punch or a blow can't really be hidden when there are no doors to shut or blinds to pull.

There wasn't only violence against women recorded by the missionaries, however. A number of distressing accounts told of women killing their newborn babies, including an eyewitness record of a woman trying to kick her newborn into the fire. It was a half-caste baby and probably she had been violently used by a white man and there were, no doubt, any number of practical reasons to end the baby's life immediately, not least of which was that the rest of the tribe insisted on it. But I thought of the intensity of feeling after the birth of my own babies, the delicate beating of their fontanelles, the fragility of their limbs. I thought too of the African women I saw everyday in Paris when I lived there during my year of Imaginary Life. Their babies were tied to their backs with red and gold and emerald slings, the gorgeous fabrics matching their long loose dresses, the babies' tiny heads bobbing as their mothers bent down to pick up green bananas at the market near Chateau Rouge. All day, every day, their babies were as near as their own skin.

I don't want to pick up my skirts and swish around with a pursed mouth like a missionary's wife, condemning the Wiradjuri mothers as barbarous as if I knew nothing of the agenda of the note-takers, but it appears there was a degree of violence in Wiradjuri culture that had less to do with the invaders and more to do with a subsistence way of life. Those who were marred in some way, too old or handicapped or of uncertain lineage, were a liability.

I had wanted to find evidence that I was connected to the Wiradjuri, not necessarily by blood, but by our shared living on the same land. I wanted to know something of their minds and hearts, their inner life before my ancestors arrived. Who were they? I remembered again the pleasure I took in the stone axes my father found on the farm and how I thought they were valuable. I loved to look at them and to touch them. I had imagined the skilful hands that made them, wondered how they had been shaped and smoothed and whether the axe-heads had ever had handles. I had run my finger along the edge of the sharpest one and tried chopping with it and made a rough nick in the gum down by the creek. If they had been axes from anywhere else, I would not have had more than a passing interest in them. I realise now they were sacred relics for me, like saints' bones for medieval pilgrims, giving connection by sight and touch.

Even so, I wanted to know that the Wiradjuri were not only interested in using their axes to find enough food and to protect themselves from the mysterious forces of evil. Perhaps it was a futile search; perhaps their ancient tribal consciousness was too different to mine.

And then, one afternoon in the Library, in the midst of looking through the inadequate records under the high ceiling of the nineteenth-century temple of knowledge, I suddenly realised that is probably what we are all doing all the time – from the dawn of human time – in all our 'after food-gathering' activities: ochre cave paintings of bison or kangaroo, Gregorian chanting, Tibetan ritual, Zoroastrian dance, Zulu masks, totems, television, drugs, alcohol, religion, art, shopping, academic research, war. After finding enough food, we try, uselessly enough, all of us, to protect ourselves from the mysterious and terrifying forces of evil. Or even more frightening than evil, the vast void beneath and on either side of breathing life, the infinite place my childhood nightmare had opened up to me and that had come swooping in like a dark bird the moment I faltered in manufacturing the story of myself.

And that, of course, is where the missionaries properly

came into the picture. That was their sole business, protecting themselves and their congregation from the mysterious forces of evil, saving benighted souls caught in superstition. Until I found their diaries I had known nothing about the missionaries apart from their names: Watson, Günther, Handt, Porter.

The missionaries didn't think the Wiradjuri had a spiritual life. They had not heard of the Dreamtime or the Rainbow Serpent and dismissed the stories they were told as fantastical. Two hundred years later, the Dreamtime has become a cultural artefact to promote Australia to the rest of the world.

While I was living in Paris, I saw an Aboriginal painting in the Musée du Quai Branly. It was called *Le Temps du Rêve*, The Time of the Dreaming. The painting had a yellow ochre background and was covered in swirls of tiny red ochre dots. I don't remember the name of the artist, but the painting was from Papunya in the Western Desert of Central Australia, thousands of kilometres from Wiradjuri country. As far as I know, everywhere throughout Australia the structure and purpose of traditional Indigenous imagery remains the same: spiritual life and country are indivisible. Paintings and stories are not intended as aesthetic experiences, but as maps, records and stories.

When I saw this painting and the others from Arnhem Land and the carved pukumani poles from the Tiwi Islands in the post-modern museum on the banks of the Seine, I felt proud. These were the artworks from my place! Through the long narrow windows I could see the museum garden and the pearl sky of Paris, one window revealing the severe beauty of the Eiffel Tower. I realise now that it was the pride of a colonial child, pleased that her parents approved of her new home in the Antipodes enough to display her art in their elegant house.

But now I think of the bora trees at Wellington. All that is left of them are the drawings of the carved patterns sketched by John Henderson in 1829. The sketches are of a ground plan of the 'temple' and of twenty-eight tree trunks, each one carved with different symbols. Most of these are recognisable from other works of ancient and contemporary Aboriginal art – wavy lines, dots, semicircles, concentric rings. But there are other less-used symbols such as rectangles and V-shapes and what look like human parts – a heart and a vulva. The patterns are beautiful. I can't stop staring at Henderson's drawings, even though I know Wiradjuri women were not allowed to see the original carvings.

I wish the bora trees had not been destroyed. I wish I could see them. They were gradually chopped down then burned, the last one, I believe, within my lifetime. If the choice were offered me between the carved trees standing on plinths, uprooted and alone, open to every gaze in the Musée du Quai Branly thousands of miles from home, and what actually happened to the bora trees from my childhood town – burned to ash – I know I would choose the indignity of them being transported across the world. It feels wrong to wish that, but I do. It's this kind of thinking that makes me realise that my mind is European, the mind of a thief.

12

The Missionaries' Diaries

I have not been the only thief.

Ngunguda nilla buranu ngaddunu; minyamminyambul ngumdia-girrin. This sentence in the Wiradjuri language was written in 1839 when the Reverend James Günther compiled a Wiradjuri–English Dictionary, much of it copied from the Reverend William Watson's notes. The purpose of the dictionary was to teach other missionaries the Wiradjuri language in order to convert the Natives to Christianity. After the standard sections on nouns and verbs and other grammar, there's a section of 'useful sentences'. The English translation of this sentence is: *Give me that child and I will give you plenty to eat.*

When I came upon the words in Günther's dictionary in the Mitchell Library, it stopped me in my tracks, the transaction so clear and simple. It was just a sentence in a dictionary stored for nearly 200 years on dim shelves, and perhaps not enough to convict, but there was plenty of other incriminating evidence in the journals. The Church Missionary Society, which appointed and funded the mission, still holds 905 pages of handwritten papers from the Wellington Valley missionaries: William Watson, Johann Handt, James Günther and catechist-agriculturalist, William Porter.

As I read their journals, the nineteenth-century grammar and phrasing lulling me, it felt as if I were swimming back through their bloodstreams and looking out through their eyes – a time traveller's view of my own country's past. I became addicted to their words. I felt as if they were letting me use their gaze, giving me direct access to the daily life of the first few years of the place that I came from. Even more than that, they gave me the pleasure of meeting individual Wiradjuri, real people with names and personalities: Kabbarrin, Rachael, Bobby, Jemmy, Bungarri and more, each of them living and breathing and arguing the point.

Watson, an Englishman in his early thirties, and Handt, a German Lutheran several years older, both employed by the Anglican Church Missionary Society, arrived in the Wellington Valley on 3 October 1832. The journey, which takes me five and a half hours, with a quick break for coffee in Bathurst, took them forty-five days. It appeared the journey alone was a challenge to their Christian faith. Their horses were skittish and broke traces and shafts, a snow storm in the Blue Mountains meant they couldn't even light a fire at night to keep warm, a dray was balanced precariously over a cliff on Victoria Pass. There was no road after Bathurst so they were frequently lost, bogged in marshes, had their drays broken, and lost their cattle and horses. At least once they arrived in the Wellington Valley there was shelter, the huts left by the soldiers and convicts.

From their journals it's evident the missionaries were idealistic personalities, the steel of their religion framing and determining all their responses. To them, the Wiradjuri were not a people to be subdued, but souls to be saved. They had more direct, daily interactions with the Wiradjuri than most other whites at the time and recorded what they saw in their diaries each day. Theirs are the only records of individual names and personalities of Wiradjuri men and women from the early years of settlement; people and moments and conversations saved from forgetfulness.

From the diary of Reverend William Watson 1832

29 Sept

As I pass'd by a Station today, an Overseer told me that we were going to Wellington on a very needless errand, for the Blacks would only laugh at us. I made answer to him. Is that any new thing? Is it strange to find persons dispos'd to laugh at religion and sacred things?

4 Oct [Arrival in the Wellington Valley]

Last night as we had not an opportunity of putting up our bed stead, we attempted to sleep on the floor, but the attempt was in vain, we were attacked with such a host of vermin.

This evening about 9 O'Clock I heard a loud screaming in the Bush at a short distance from our house. At first I thought it proceeded from some children quarrelling, but when I arrived at the place from which it proceeded I found King Bogin beating his wife in a most cruel manner.

He has cut her arm to the bone and lacerated her head and right side very severely. I prevailed on him to cease but he was very angry, and having emptied her bag of the trinkets which they usually carry with them he threw it at her, as he did also some water 3 times (I suppose as a deed of separation) and then told her to go away deeper into the Bush to make a fire for herself, for he would have nothing more to do with her, but the creature could scarcely crawl and it rained very heavily and was exceedingly dark.

11 Nov

Alas how little love do I feel towards him whose sufferings and death are set forth in such a striking manner in these emblems. What are ordinances but empty channels when the Spirit of God is absent, when the love of X't [Christ] is not felt or his glory seen. How ill qualified surely must I be for recommending the love of X't [Christ] to others, while I am destitute of it myself.

4 Dec

Several Black children came from Goboleon today. I taught them letters by marking them out with pipeclay on a board, let each of them have a slate and a piece of pipeclay to make letters themselves. They were much entertained with looking at my pictures.

They come over every Sunday and occasionally during the week. It is a great treat to them to sit down in my study and look at the books. Scarcely anything surprises the Blacks more than to see my library. They never saw so many books together before.

There is intellectual acuteness enough in them. Indeed I have never found any deficiency of it in reference to things with which they are acquainted, so far is the charge of idiotism proffered against them wide off the truth. The period may be distant, but I have no doubt it will come, when it shall please God to change their hearts when they will equal if not outvie some of the now civilised and polished nations of Europe.

The weather is extremely hot here. Thermometer yesterday 94 in the shade. In the sun 120.

6 Dec

At this station I saw Rachael [sic], the gin to Bobby King of Wellington, who expects every hour to be delivered. She was in the hut and attended by a Black female and an old man whom they name the Doctor. She was here a short time ago and I warned her not to kill the child when it should be born, she promised me that she would not. The man at the hut informs me that several Blacks (whether male or female I cannot say) persuaded her to go into the Bush that the child might be destroyed as soon as it made its appearance, that she refused, saying parson 'tell her not tumble it down, he be murra cooley (very angry) if she did'. He says they threatened to spear her if she would not, and so they prevailed.

8 Dec

Two Black gins came over from Kelley's very early this morning, but not before I had heard that Rachael had murdered her child. I asked them about it, they enquired who told me, but that I was not disposed to answer. They acknowledged that the child had been murdered and they said that too by Kelley. I have been told today what I fear is too true, that Kelley pays to King Bobby a certain portion of handkerchiefs &c for the loan of Rachael, and this child was his.

13 Dec

Kelley came today to have his eye dressed (as he has done occasionally for a long time). I spoke to him in plain terms in reference to his connexion with Rachael and the very great guilt which must attach to such conduct. I told what I had heard. He denied its being true, he said the child was 'still born', however I gave him to understand that I firmly believed what I had heard. I had another circumstance against him, he had been beating in a most severe and cruel manner one of the Black gins who is old. What are my feelings at the conduct of these English stock-keepers may be better conceived than described.

1833

21 April

Our children respond very well at church. I am sometimes almost ready to imagine myself at St Mary's, Islington, when I hear them. They are very partial to singing, indeed all the Natives are very much attracted by music. They are almost ready to dance at the sound of the flute.

27 April

When we had come near to the place we perceived by the light of the fire a white infant laid very near to it, and apparently struggling in the agonies of death but not crying. The elder yeener was sitting with her back to it, and the younger yeener was digging a hole in the ground with a long stick (which they use for the purpose of digging up roots &c). Mrs W asked her why she had killed the child? She said no good that one, this one very good, taking the Black child Charlotte and putting it to her breast. Mrs W asked her if she killed the child with the staff? She said no, with her foot. Mrs W took the babe and wrapped it in a blanket which she took from one of the girls, and folded it in her cloak for it is a very severely frosty night.

30 June

We have generally some sick and occasionally from half a dozen to a dozen [Aborigines] at the same time apparently destined to an early dissolution, filthy and corrupt in their bodies through the ravages of the venereal, covered with sores &c and unwilling to move from their place on any account, or to do anything for themselves. I must wash and dress their wounds, their victuals must be prepared for and taken to them. Under such circumstances it will be readily conceived that we must be attacked by a host of vermin as well as be affected with the most unpleasant stench.

1834

1 Jan

A man came over from Goboleon to say that seven armed bushrangers had robbed a hut at a short distance and had intimated their intention of coming to Wellington. We have indeed more danger to apprehend from such characters than from the untutored Natives around us.

4 July

One of the boys observed 'I believe all children go to Heaven'.

I said they are not baptised.

He then remarked 'What for all pikininny go to fire, no good that'.

1835

2 Feb

41 natives here this morning, 22 of them came to breakfast. I had last night prepared some boiled Wheat and Beef, so when they came up I was ready to distribute the same to them. I embraced the opportunity this afford of addressing them; the Lord grant it may be for the good. Most of them immediately left the Establishment . . .

16 July

Mrs Watson has been confined to her bed through sickness for two or three days – the child is likewise very ill, always in the cradle unable to sit up and as I have no assistance but my little girls who are by no means attached to the infant, I have had it to wash and dress and otherwise attend to, as well as to Mrs Watson and to cook for a large number of Natives, my hands and heart and head have been fully engaged.

20 Sept

Reading in my tent today, and only 3 natives present, an Old native said 'do not be miserable, do not be miserable: don't you want to be in the house at Wellington?' I should be always happy, and I wanted the natives also to go there . . .

26 Sept

King Bungarri one of our native boys was sitting in the garden resting himself to day. Seeing him busily employed I went up to him and found that having moistened some clay, he had made a very striking image of a child, or woman in miniature, calling it a 'Lolly' (Doll). It was well proportioned, and its large Bonnet with knotts [sic] of ribbons on it looked very well. He afterwards made a gig and Horse with all the things necessary for drawing and placed his 'Lolly' in the Gig. When it shall please the Lord to convert these native by His Holy Spirit they will develope [sic] intellectual powers, far beyond what many at present, are willing to acknowledge them possessed of.

3 Oct

This is our third anniversary in this lonely wild. A wild it was when we entered on it, and a wild it remains. No real improvement appears in the general conduct of the natives. They are as wicked in every point of view as they were before our arrival. Several have died during the year in the Bush, of whom who can say that they have gone to heaven? We have need indeed to humble ourselves deeply before our God. While the emissaries of Satan are successful at all points, we have too much reason to take up the lamentation of the prophet, and say 'I have laboured in vain, and spent my strength for nought and in vain'. Several times when there appeared a breaking in the clouds, and we were hoping to see light arising out of darkness, suddenly the clouds became thicker and darker and we were left to bemoan our false calculations. Again and again this has been the case with us, so that now we are afraid to hope.

6 Oct

They always say our speaking to them respecting their evil conduct, is being angry. Many times when I have been endeavouring to show them the danger of a sinful course, they have said 'speak good' 'speak good' 'don't speak that way'.

17 October

Had some conversation with the natives here this evening; as usual Kabbarrin was the chief speaker. He said that when he sees a shooting star it is the departing Spirit of some native, (others say it is an omen of the death of some native) that the soul also makes a buzzing noise when it first leaves the body. He said many curious and superstitious things which nothing but a knowledge of the gospel will eradicate.

Gungin is sadly out of order to night . . . I remarked that he was running about all the day, not doing any thing for us, nor under any instruction. He replied in a very fiery manner. What do you want here? What do you come here for? Why do you not go to your own country.

19th Dec

I remarked that the great Spirit whom we name God was the maker of all things. He enquired 'What God?' 'I believe white man made the Bible and then put down God in it.' 'O Baiami is a great Doctor, parson is no Doctor.'

1836

19 June

Kabbarrin refused to have his jacket this morning, a good new blue one for which I lately paid 16/- in Bathurst, he says that it looks too much like 'new chum' a name given to newly arrived assigned servants.

25 July

Kabbarrin has been dreaming again. He says that last night he saw the Lord, who put his hand on Kabbarrin's head, he saw many cords let down from heaven far whiter and more beautiful than any he ever saw before. He says that he also saw that very dark place.

29 Aug

It has often occurred to my mind that the existence in their Dialect of a word for shame, and the frequent use of it among them, is an evidence that, though guilty of every vice that can disgrace human nature, they yet profess a higher sense of moral propriety than people imagine, or than we could easily believe considering their general licentious behaviour. Indeed some of their regulations, or customs, are truly admirable as it regards modesty.

16 Nov

What then was my astonishment, on coming from the Bush about 6 o'clock this evening, to see about two hundred, near the mission house, standing in battle array with all their weapons of war, their spears pointed, and ready for an attack. The number of our natives present was very small. I told them that this ground was sacred, and no fighting could be permitted. But they appeared deaf to all I said. One apparently full of self importance, had much to say respecting his having been at Bathurst, – how Englishmen did when men were brought before a magistrate – how the land 'all about' belonged to the natives, and that I was not to mind.

I was therefore more determined to let them know that I was a peacemaker. I had to ride up and down the ranks of the enemy, and occasionally to knock down a spear already pointed: while our own natives were continually calling out 'Mr Watson keep at outside the spears will hit you – the Bargans will hit you.' However I hazarded the danger and succeeded in preventing any fighting at that time; but not before I was so hoarse with shouting that I could scarcely speak . . . I spoke to them respecting religion: some listened, and, asked questions: others laughed. Some said that 'they did not understand about soul; but they understand tobacco and pipes'.

17 Nov

The natives came up this morning promising to be peaceable. I endeavoured to impress, upon their minds, the truths of religion; but they had no ears for those things, they were hungry and wanted food. In the afternoon seeing some

natives running up from the river, and from that infer-
ring that all was not right, I immediately mounted my
horse and rode up, when I found them engaged in hot
war: their poisoned spears were flying in all directions,
and their tremendous clubs were in full play. One of our
Natives (Charley) had his skull fractured and part of his
brain appeared in the hair: his ribs were also much bruised;
however I instantly rushed in among them, and after much
to do, succeeded in stopping the engagement.

27 Feb

The mothers of our new come children are continually
teasing us to give them up; but knowing that if let alone
the dear little creatures will be happy enough, we shall not
easily surrender them.

From the diary of Reverend James Günther 1837

August 9

In catechising the Children today I was much pleased and
surprised at the progress they have made, not only in reading the English, but also in Scriptural knowledge. Some of
them would put many European children to shame. However degraded they may be, they afford at least a decisive
proof, that they are quite as capable of cultivation of the
mind as other nations.

16 Aug

I copied a number of words today from a vocabulary of
Mr Watson's of the Aboriginal language. From the little I

have seen and heard of this language, during the few days of my residence here, I conclude that it is not so poor as we might naturally expect, judging from their rude manner of living, in consequence of which their notions must be very confined.

Was much pleased this evening with Fredric, one of our Native youths, apparently a very droll fellow, saying his prayers so well in English or rather leading the rest of the Youths & Children.

21 August
In the afternoon when several Native women were standing before my Study door waiting for a frock which Mrs G. was making for one of them, I read some sentences to them in Wirradurri when they amused themselves in correcting & teaching me.

10 Sept
It must be allowed that the men are not quite so vile as the females who become wives or prostitutes at so early an age.

25 Sept
Mrs G. performed an operation to day, which amused & surprised me, she was cutting the hair of one of our Black youths a very robust & tall fellow called George. I was surprised that Mrs G. had inclination & ability for it for it was a very nasty job; the Blacks exhale commonly a smell which is almost intolerable when you come near them. Besides the young man had just been greasing his hair with fish-fat as they frequently do. The poor fellow was quite

proud of having his hair cut by Mrs G. thanked her very much and would say, it was done 'Capital'.

In the evening we were highly amused by this very young man and another Jemmy who had been fishing & were very lucky. In less than an hour they caught from 15 to 18 fishes all from about 3 to 6 pounds weight, one they caught which we estimated to weigh nearly twenty. They were very liberal with them both to us & the Natives. When they observed our surprise & delight they were highly gratified and laughed all the time.

28 Sept

Mrs G. gave this morning a reading lesson to some of the Black youths on the Establishment, Jemmy, George & Harry, who have taken a fancy to learn reading. When they had done reading or rather spelling they desired Mrs G. to teach them to sing also.

29 Sept

We had hardly done breakfast when Mrs G's. pupils made their appearance desirous to read. When reading was over I gave my singing lesson, in the same way as yesterday.

1839

May 25

I was much amused & struck with some observations of Cochrane's to day. A certain Individual whose vanity & self conceit attract the notice of most persons, passed by, with so much consequence, that our poor heathen youth could not forbear expressing his disgust & observed: 'That fellow very proud; No body so proud as that man, he think he magistrate etc etc' adding very significantly: 'I believe that fellow not know his heart.' This evidently shows that C. is aware of the close connection of self-knowledge & humility.

1840
April 3
Besides teaching the few Youths that are remaining occasionally I am still pursuing the study of the language, and have endeavoured yesterday & to day to translate the Lord's Prayer, into it; not without some difficulty, since, what we should call essential words, are lacking in this language. But some of my most intelligent young men approve of my translation, calling it correct & intelligible.

25 Dec
This was a poor Christmas day indeed! How distressing & discouraging! No body at Church but our two White men and about half a dozen Blacks . . . Our Aboriginal youths were in a very bad careless mood determined to run away to the Camp immediately after Service and laughed at all my warnings & exhortations. When I spoke of leaving them Bungary [Bungarri] replied: 'Well you may, we know now enough.' This is in a great measure the fruit of all that has passed on this Mission so disgraceful to the Good Cause. They know to take advantage of it; a short time since when I warned Bungary against having any thing to do with a certain worthless treacherous Aborigine, he replied: 'We are not like Missionaries, we love one another.' What one's

feeling must be under such circumstances our friends may imagine.

From the Diary of Brother Johann Handt
1832

24 Nov

Asked some black women this evening who were sitting around the fire, where their children were but they replied, why I asked for their children . . . I told them however that we desired to instruct their children, and to make them like ourselves, after which they replied that they had no children.

Date unknown

They are instructed as opportunity presents itself, at home, in the bush or in the camp, by talking, or reading a passage of Scripture, or delivering a short discourse to them, in their own language. Their attention is not always to be gained, as they are frequently given to much talk and jest.

From the Diary of William Porter
1838

31 July

They are a great deal more inclined to read than to work; being naturally the most indolent people in the world.

13

More Inclined to Read than Work

As I finally clicked off the online journals, I imagined the missionaries writing in the evenings by lamp light, sitting at a desk with an ink pot, pens, blotter, describing their activities, making their observations of the Wiradjuri, pouring out their disappointments and their bitterness against each other. They must have heard the evening sounds of my childhood – crickets chirruping, mopokes calling mournfully, frogs croaking and booming from the river, mosquitoes buzzing – but they don't mention any of them.

I liked Watson recording the temperature and the weather; I liked Günther's surprise at his wife giving one of the Wiradjuri men a haircut – I could feel his awareness of the intimacy of such an act. I laughed out loud at Watson's indignation with Kabbarrin not wanting to wear the good new blue jacket he'd lately paid sixteen shillings for in Bathurst. Watson clearly didn't know anything about style.

Mostly though, the journals had the same effect on me as

the religious arguments I used to have with my father when I was a teenager. For a while I'd make the mistake of thinking we, my father and I, were rationally debating the issue around the kitchen table, but the argument always ended when his evidence became, 'God says.' With me on one side and God on the other, I didn't stand a chance. That's why I'm impressed with Kabbarrin's argument on the question of how a God is constructed: 'What God? I believe white man made the Bible and then put down God in it.' Why didn't I think of saying that?

And Bungarri's quick, sharp dig at the missionaries' failure to follow the central teaching of Christianity: 'We are not like the missionaries, we love one another.' By that stage Günther and Watson could not stand each other and for one of the Natives to assume superiority in understanding Christian charity must have been more than irritating. I can see the innocent look on Bungarri's face as he so precisely sticks the knife in.

And even an eight-year-old child could point out the injustice of the unutterably cruel concept of hell: 'What for all pikininny go to fire, no good that.' Of course it was no bloody good. I remember trying to accommodate the concept of hell when I was about twelve by deciding if I had to believe it existed then it must be uninhabited.

I was impressed too with Gungin arguing the politics of ownership and respect and identity – 'What do you want here? What do you come here for? Why do you not go to your own country.' And again, another unnamed man, 'apparently full of self-importance', according to Watson, argued that 'The land all about belonged to natives and he (Watson) was not to mind'.

But more intriguing than all debates is the Wiradjuri

response to the obstinate, one-tracked nagging of the missionaries. Even through the missionaries' eyes, and even despite their frequent wars with other tribes, the Wiradjuri seem to have been, as a culture, extraordinarily good-humoured. They come across as laconic, easy-going blokes, laughing and joking, a bit puzzled that the missionaries never seemed to get it. When I read of their 'jesting' and 'drollery' and laughter and sardonic comments, I envied their ease in letting the missionaries' many and various manias slide off their fish-oiled skin.

The parsons preached and scolded, were stiff and spiky, angry and miserable. They worried about sex and swearing and stealing and indolence and disobeying the Sabbath, they bickered and argued bitterly among themselves – and they tore their souls apart about why the Natives didn't want to be like them. The Wiradjuri took the meat and bread and tobacco offered, listened politely for a while, shed tears when the missionaries told moving stories, tried to be accommodating to these obviously unhappy people, attempted to persuade them not to speak so harshly, and then tried to jolly them along with their high-spirited enjoyment of life.

What might have really tried the patience of the Wiradjuri – it certainly started to annoy me – was the missionaries' constant turning of all situations and conversations towards sin and evil, especially the evil of illicit sex, which they mostly blamed on the licentious nature of the 'women', often little girls in fact, and on the Aboriginal men who traded their wives so freely. For the missionaries, it wasn't so much a matter of age or exploitation, but that unmarried sex was sinful, full stop. Which is why it is so neatly paradoxical that it was this sin, committed by one of the missionaries themselves, that finally brought the mission undone. Shockingly, and worse, embarrassingly, it was discovered that William Porter, the catechist, had been having sex with one of the Aboriginal mission women for at least two years!

Poor Mr Porter had tried for some time to persuade the Mission Society to pay for his fiancée to come from England but the society refused. His sexual relationship with the Aboriginal woman began at the time of the final refusal. What galled the other missionaries the most was that the Aborigines now had a 'handle against one of our members'. It must have been excruciating to be so caught out, laughed at by their naked congregation.

I don't think the missionaries were evil, just misled by doctrine and a desire for influence and by their own stiff-necked personalities. Doctrine distorted their view, made sin appear where there was none, or worse, made the real sins invisible. The missionaries told themselves they simply wanted to save the Natives' eternal souls, but there is so much frustration in their journal entries at their lack of influence over the local Wiradjuri that it has to be read as thwarted desire for power. Why else be annoyed that Gungin didn't want to be ordered about by them; why else be so upset that the girls working for them wanted to return to the bush; why else keep stealing Wiradjuri children? There are entries over and over again bewailing the fruitlessness of the missionaries' efforts. A successful missionary has a great deal of power over minds and bodies but the Wellington Valley missionaries were, to their unending chagrin, unable to gain any real power over the Wiradjuri. The Wiradjuri just weren't interested.

In the end, it is Porter's remark I like the best of any of the journal entries: 'They are a great deal more inclined to read than to work; being naturally the most indolent people in the world.'

I laughed aloud when I first read it. At least, along with all their nagging, the missionaries had given the Wiradjuri a love of reading, opening up the sublime possibilities of a vast world. And more importantly for me, they had given them a desire I could recognise. Like them, I am a great deal more inclined to read than to work. For that I am willing to forgive the missionaries a multitude of their sins.

I have no memory whatsoever of learning to read. I do remember sitting at a wooden kindergarten desk in our one-room school with a book open in front of me, impatiently waiting because *I* had finished it already. Reading was like breathing; it was impossible not to do it and I've been addicted to it for longer than memory will allow. I do remember learning to read in French, real reading that is, not just painfully trying to force meaning word by word from the obstinate page in my high school French class, but actually relishing the juice of narrative. It happened suddenly one evening after I had already been in Paris for six months. The pedantic little cipher that insisted on exact definition must have suddenly slipped, allowing me to fall, surprised, into the joyful stream of meaning.

I suppose it was something like that for Kabbarrin and Gungin and all the other Wiradjuri youths when they learned to read. But they were not only learning to read in a foreign language as I was, and not only in an unknown script, but without any previous knowledge that black marks on a page could yield a story, could make a voice speak inside your head. It was an extraordinary leap to realise there was sound and colour and action inside those black squiggles in the missionaries' books. And then to learn what the squiggles meant. There had to be an enticement and that, of course, was the fabulous stories: battles between brothers, warring tribes, rains of fire, seas parting, messages carved on stone, wanderings in the desert, heads of seers on plates, wise elders making decrees, spirit creatures ascending and descending on ladders from the skies – they must have all made sense to the Wiradjuri. It was only natural they had the desire to learn to read the stories for themselves.

Reading created in me the desire to see the carved faces under the Pont Neuf – I had read about them in Victor Hugo's *Hunchback of Notre Dame*; to walk past Gertrude Stein's house in the rue Fleurus – I had read of her soirées in Ernest Hemingway's *A Movable Feast*; to stare in the window of Picasso's Bateau Lavoir at the end of my street – I'd read about it in Stein's *An Autobiography of Alice B. Toklas*; to lounge in Café de Flore – I had read Simone de Beauvoir's *The Mandarins*; to shiver in the cool air in narrow, cobbled Left Bank alleys – I had read Émile Zola's *Therese Raquin* and Honoré de Balzac's *Père Goriot*. Black marks on white pages created the desire to live in those streets and breathe in that air, making them far more real than the unwritten world around me.

Apart from a couple of local histories, which can be bought at the Historical Museum, there are no books written about Wellington. The Wiradjuri stories have been lost or hidden in museums, and we are all bereft.

14

Living at Nanima Reserve

It was several weeks since I had talked to Joyce. When I rang her again one of her grandchildren answered the phone.

'She's out on the veranda,' he said.

I heard him calling out and the sound of a screen door opening and shutting before Joyce picked up the receiver.

'I'm coming up again this week, Joyce. Have you got any time free?'

'Okay. Give me a ring when you get 'ere.'

'Can I make a time to see you now?'

'Nah, give me a ring when you're 'ere.'

I put the phone down, unsure whether I had an appointment to see her or not.

After I arrived in Wellington, I booked into a cabin in the caravan park on the Macquarie River. It was aluminium with bare walls, but it did have a small veranda looking down to the fast-flowing river. The long drought had broken over the last couple of months and the brown water foamed around branches tangled in the roots of magnificent old river gums that must have sheltered Wiradjuri before any of my ancestors ever came here. I unpacked and draped my clothes over chairs. I wondered if Joyce would actually talk to me or whether I'd come on a wild goose chase.

The next morning I rang her and asked if I could come around. She agreed as if we had already settled on a date and time. I looked through my clothes. I didn't want to dress too casually and have Joyce think I was not treating her with proper respect, but at the same time I didn't want to be too 'flash'. In my family it doesn't do to be 'flash'. It's read as a sign that you think you are better than other people, one of the toffs. As kids, we had one outfit of 'town clothes' each and the rest of the time wore whatever we could find in the old kitchen dresser that served as a closet in the unlined passageway. In photographs taken at home, we look like hillbillies from the Depression era with our oversized shorts, short-armed shirts, tight jackets wrongly buttoned, bare feet, hair chopped in a basin cut; there was no chance anyone would mistake us for toffs. I put on my linen skirt and brown top patterned with Chinese writing, quiet and tidy-looking.

As I drew up outside Joyce's house and climbed out of the car with my bag of books and micro recorder, a black woman appeared at the door of the neighbouring house. I glanced over. Perhaps I was considered an intruder here.

'Hallo,' she said shyly.

'G'day,' I said, and then felt embarrassed.

An ordinary innocent Aussie, that's me. The neighbour nodded and disappeared.

I unlatched Joyce's gate and walked up the cement path.

The front garden was nondescript, a bush or two, but infinitely neater than the one I grew up in. Our yard was bare dirt with scattered marshmallow grass and, later, a few small patches of lawn that tried to stay alive through droughts. We had a cracked fibro lavatory patched with tin, a mud hut housing the generator, and three long clotheslines stretching from one chicken-wire fence to the other. Our handed-down toys were scattered about, holes were dug here and there for various games, chooks wandered in and were chased out. My mother swept the dirt with a straw broom in an occasional attempt at tidiness. We knew we were poor, but both my mother with her disrespectful Irish attitude and my father with his devotion to religion made us feel we were superior for not having material burdens.

Joyce's front door was open so I knocked on the frame of the gauze screen. When Joyce came up the hall and opened the screen my first impression was of perfect neatness. I had dressed correctly, a small critic in my brain breathed more easily. She was small, with curly white hair framing a brown face, observant, friendly eyes. She wore a pastel floral top of the sort that old ladies often wear – she was eighty-four, she told me again, although she looked much younger – and neatly cut navy blue shorts that came to her knees.

'Oh, it's so nice to have a visitor,' she said, smiling widely, as if I was doing her a favour instead of being one of a long line of white people imposing on her time.

She led me down the hall into a dim room dominated by a table covered in a heavy cloth. There was little other furniture apart from a filing cabinet and a sideboard, but there were a number of photographs and what looked liked framed awards on the sideboard. The walls were lined with a soft chipboard – the material used for noticeboards that thumb-tacks can be pressed into. Bits of it were gouged out here and there and it was in need of a coat of paint, but the impression was still one of striking neatness.

I have to explain myself here. It sounds as if I'm saying, 'my goodness, isn't it wonderful that some of these Natives can be so neat', when I'm trying to say, 'this is so different to my childhood home'. In our house, beds were rarely made, mountains of dirty clothes lined the tin-roofed alleyway between the bedrooms and living room, kitchen cupboards overflowed with sticky tins and jars. There was no system for getting rid of household rubbish, unless grabbing the empty golden syrup tins and sauce bottles and hurling them over the chook yard fence can be called a system.

It's not that we weren't well cared for – we ate roast lamb and apple pie, wore clean, ironed clothes to town at least – best clothes for church and last year's best for anything else – and had ample love and freedom; it's just that my mother seemed to not be interested in running an orderly household – and with eight children, that sort of attitude was always going to result in vast and general mess. She laughed at her lack of house-keeping skills and expected us to have the same disrespect for women whose main interest was a tidy house. My mother was definitely one of those people who were so indolent they would rather read than work. Even now in her retirement village, she explained the oddness of her neighbour by leaning over and quietly confiding, 'I think she is one of those people who are very neat.' To my mother, striking neatness was a sign of someone who had a possibly disturbing grasp on the world.

Joyce gestured for me to sit down at the table. We were both ready to head straight into it. Starting with Joyce meant I was starting with the claim of family, a connection, however tenuous, between the Wiradjuri and my own past. She had told me her grandfather and my great grandmother were brother and sister; that must count for something.

'Where were you born?' I started.

'In a corrugated iron hut at Nanima. My grandmother, Granny May, delivered me. Everyone called her Granny May – she delivered all the babies born at Nanima and at Blacks Camp on the Common. She was married to John May, but he was called Farbie May.'

'She was the midwife?'

'Yeah. Delivered all the babies. I was born twenty-fourth November 1926, an' called Joyce Marguerite Riley. My mother was called Maggie May.'

'Maggie May! Like the song.'

'Yeah.'

Joyce gestured towards a large photograph with an old-fashioned frame hanging on the wall above the filing cabinet. I stood up and walked over to have a better look at it. A young Maggie May was sitting in a cane chair, wearing a loose Chinese-looking dress and holding a fan. She was dark-skinned with European features and a gentle, almost timid, manner. According to Joyce, she was my grandfather Frank's cousin. I wondered if he ever knew her.

'So you reckon Farbie May's sister was my dad's grand-mother, Rosina?'

'That's right. He was born out at Murrumbidgerie. Near Guerie.'

'And their mother was Lauannah or Lavinia? In our records, we are not sure which.'

'Laureena.'

'Laureena?'

'Her name was Laureena.'

Joyce was adamant, no question about it. I hadn't heard of any Laureena. I needed to check that.

'And Laureena was dark?'

'Yeah, she was dark. I got a sort of memory of sittin' in the park when I was a little girl next to Laureena. She was a big black woman wearing a black lacy-lookin' hat.'

I could see her easily: a plump Aboriginal woman in a fancy hat on the grass in Cameron Park where the Aborigines always hung around when I was a child. It was as close as I could get to the woman who might be my Wiradjuri ancestor. She was no more than a vague picture in Joyce's mind, slipping and shifting over the years as memory does. Joyce could just as easily have been remembering someone else altogether.

Joyce had a brother born two years later, Bill, the one I'd met, and an older sister, Eileen, who had died when she was eleven years old after she was accidentally bumped by a boy in the playground and hit her head against the wall of the school. There was another little boy who died, Joyce didn't know how, and two little sisters, one dead from bronchitis when she was a toddler and the other from convulsions brought on by a cat scratching her face on the day of the first one's funeral.

'Four of your mother's children dead! God, how terrible! How did she go on with life after that!'

'These things happened,' Joyce said.

Her no-nonsense tone reminded me of Gran Miller, the

same pragmatic attitude. Country women, black and white, must have been made of tougher stuff in those days.

'When babies died at Nanima and Blacks Camp they were put in little wooden boxes and then we put 'em in holes in the bank of the river,' Joyce went on.

'Really? Buried in the river bank?' It sounded strangely magical, babies in burrows like rows of little sleeping water-creatures, waiting perhaps to be hatched out as a platypus or river fish.

'Yeah, an' then we put big stones to stop dogs or whatever. But then, one day, a huge flood came and the coffins started to be washed away so some of the young fellas dived down into the flood and grabbed 'em. The babies were re-buried on the Common, but no-one remembers exactly where they are anymore.'

She seemed to be making a point about the babies being buried on the Common, not just telling a story. Her tone implied something I didn't understand, but I let it go as Joyce had already gone on into a complicated family history.

Joyce and her brother Bill lived with Granny and Farbie May after their father, Herbie Riley, and Maggie May split up. Their cousin, Billie May, lived with them too. His mother, Katie May, worked for a station owner who raped her on the weekends when his wife went to town to do the shopping, so she ran away on Christmas Day one year. Her family found her fifty-seven years later in Boggabri and everyone in the town celebrated.

'One day, my cousin, Ruby Riley, was taken away by the Guv'ment and ended up in Parramatta Girls Home in Sydney.'

'Oh, that's terrible. I've heard about that place.'

'So then her brother, Johnny, was claimed by his aunt and his name changed to Johnny George so he wouldn't be taken away.'

'Good idea.' I nodded.

''Cept Ruby and Johnny never found each other again. Often we knew when the Guv'ment people were coming though. Well, I didn't, I was just a kid. One mornin' very early, still dark in fact, Granny May woke me, told me to get up. But Gran, it's still dark, I said. No matter, she said, you're goin' on holiday to Peak Hill with your Auntie Thelma.'

It was more than seventy years ago but Joyce remembered the horse and sulky waiting in the dark, a lantern swinging from the backboard. She was eight years old, maybe nine, bundled onto the sulky with Auntie and a few belongings. The horse trotted away from Nanima along the dirt road. There is always a clarity travelling somewhere in the early morning; you never forget the clear, cool strangeness of it and I could see in Joyce's face the freshness of the memory, her childhood excitement. She was on holiday for two months.

'More 'an twenty-five years later, in the sixties, I was workin' at Wellington District Hospital when Auntie Thelma came in. I was helpin' her, givin' her a bit of a back rub – I wasn't a nurse, just givin' her a rub – an' Auntie said she had something to tell me. She said, Remember that holiday. The Guv'ment was comin' to take you that day. That's why you came to stay with me.'

'You were lucky.'

Joyce grinned. Clever rather than lucky, her look said. She felt well cared for even though their house was made of corrugated iron (crinkle tin, I remember Bill called it) with a dirt floor. There were only seven houses at Nanima at that time and they were all the same. The rest were on the Common where some 'outsiders from Peak Hill had arrived', Joyce told me pointedly, and a few humpies half a mile away at Blacks Camp where Granny May had been born. Most people had moved from Blacks Camp to the Nanima site in 1910. Bill Riley had told me years before that their grandfather, John Riley, had written to Queen Victoria about the flooding at Blacks Camp and she had written back advising them to seek out and establish another location, which they duly did. The letter from Queen Victoria was kept at Nanima school for most of the twentieth century, but in the 1990s some kid stole and burnt it. To Bill this was evidence of the general decay that had set in at Nanima by then.

'Our place was lined with wheat bags painted with lime,' Joyce continued. She was an easy talker. 'Still pretty cold in winter, you know the frosts 'ere in winter and too hot in summer. Early on, Granny May used ta cook on an open fire in the hearth, she 'ad a camp oven, but later on we 'ad a proper wood stove. We 'ad a bath made out of flattened kerosene tins and the water was heated in kettles on the fire.'

'We did that too,' I said, proud of it for the first time.

The steaming water would be poured into dishes for an all-over wash starting with the face and ending with the 'tail'. No-one else we knew bathed in a dish – and I made sure no-one at school found out. We didn't have running hot water, or even running cold water, until I was about ten, when my father built a kitchen and installed a tap. Before then, water had to be carried inside in kettles from the corrugated iron water tanks outside.

'We 'ad a church and a school at Nanima in my day.'

'Were there missionaries at Nanima then?'

I had thought they left after Porter's liaison with the Aboriginal woman and the mortifying close of the Mission in Wellington.

'Yeah. They lived next to the church, but they didn't run the place. Farbie ran things, if anyone did. They 'ad a tin church, painted red, and one afternoon a really big storm blew up.' She grinned. 'It was really blowy, and then I was lookin' out the window and a red sheet of tin blew past! And then another one! And another. The whole church blew away. Next mornin', all that was left was the organ.'

She chuckled, delighted by her story.

'Wow – that's amazing!'

'Yeah, just the organ sittin' there. Just the organ all by itself. And we all looked at it.'

And tried to hide their grins, by the look in Joyce's eyes all these years later. I could just see them gazing soberly at the forlorn organ, trying not to let missionaries see them laughing.

'So the missionaries left after that.' Joyce chuckled again, her engaging wicked grin lighting up her face.

She told me then about going to school, still in the era of memorising poetry, doing sums, sewing and raffia work. Miss Rose Taylor was her teacher. Another teacher, Miss Ardell, married one of the Aboriginal students, Ernest Daley, which must have given both their families something to discuss over dinner. I remember Lester Daley sat behind me in school, the only Aborigine in my class. He was nice looking, gentle and shy, and I often whispered to him in maths and borrowed his ruler. I wonder if he was a descendant of Miss Ardell and Ernest.

'I got into trouble from the teachers because some tittle-tats had told the teachers we had painted our bodies with clay down at the river. Miss Taylor said, you have to keep your bodies clean.'

I clucked sympathetically but Joyce wasn't really bothered. Her tone was not bitter or even angry, she was just telling it like it was.

'We also got inta trouble for usin' language. I only knew a few words but old Granny Jewel, Granny Stuart, Auntie Martha Daley, Bert Dempsey and Ben Harris, they could all use language and we would listen and pick up a few words. We would just say, Look at that lot of mayngs [whites] over there, and the teachers would tell us not to use those words.'

The elders also taught Joyce and the other kids traditional dancing. They would slip their shoes off and dance around a big old fire bucket in the lantern light and the kids would join in, Ned Daley in his hobnailed boots.

'One time there were six of us kids dancin', havin' a wonderful time and Granny Stuart suddenly stopped us. How many of you kids are dancin'? she asked. Six, Granny, we said. Six? said Granny. Well who owns that other shadow then? And we counted the shadows and there were seven. There's someone else dancing, said Granny.'

I had to break in at this point. 'What did Granny Stuart think it was?'

'She didn't say. She jus' said there was a shadow dancin' with us.'

★

It was time for Joyce to pick up her great grandkids from school. Time for me to go. We hadn't even started to talk about the Native Title claim although I had a fair idea that's what Joyce was hinting towards when she mentioned the families from Peak Hill living on the Common. They were the beginning of the problem, the people who didn't belong. Probably Rose's family. I couldn't hope to find out about all that in a few minutes. All Joyce's information came in the form of stories, and stories take longer than lists of facts.

As I stood up and bundled my books and tape recorder back in my bag, I tentatively asked if I could come back tomorrow. Joyce said yes immediately, as if it were no imposition at all. Then I remembered the photocopy I'd made for her from Henderson's journal, the page of drawings of the bora ground on the Macquarie River. I told her what I knew: that they were drawn by a Mr John Henderson in the late 1820s about fifteen years after the first whites arrived. I felt guilty as I handed it to her. This was all I could give – a record of what was destroyed.

'Women were not allowed to see the bora ground, were they?'

'No, that's right.' She grinned, seemingly not bothered that we were both breaking an old law. 'And the men weren't allowed to be at the birthing places.'

'Do you know where they were, these trees?' I asked.

'No,' she said. 'Maybe out Bodangara way. There's a lot of axes and things out that way.'

'I think they might have been closer,' I said. 'I'll find out if I can and I will tell you straightaway.'

It was stupid making a promise when I had no idea if I could fulfil it, but it seemed necessary to at least try to make reparation.

15

Thieving Ancestors

I didn't feel like going back to the cabin so I decided to drive out to Nanima to see what it was like these days. It was the same road I had come on nearly thirty years ago but where was the alien landscape I had remembered? It wasn't dry or harsh at all. The paddocks were knee deep in ripe grasses, creamy and golden with new green growth tingeing it with freshness, the slopes of the hills were gentle, the sky a soft blue scattered with puffy clouds. Except for the gumtrees it could have been a late summer landscape in the south of France. Even the native pines on Pine Hill looked delicate and soft.

When I crested the hill, I couldn't see anything over the pines so I kept on driving, thinking I would pull over when I caught sight of the Mission and just observe it from a distance, but I kept going, down through a small herd of horses, over the cattle ramp and into the cluster of houses. The village didn't look the same as I remembered either. There were about twenty-five buildings lining the T which made up the shape of the settlement; some were fibro, the older ones, but most were brick and some had cultivated gardens, one crowded with bright red, green and yellow gnomes and other cement garden creatures. There was a broken fibro church with a sign, 'Nanima Shalom Church', which looked like it had not been used for years, and a closed shop.

I drove back to the cabin and sat out on the veranda in the river-cooled air. I thought about my father's stories of going to visit his grandmother Rosina in her dirt-floored hut and wondered if they could be true. It sounded like Nanima but it seemed most unlikely that she lived there because she was married to Charlie Miller, who had a homestead on top of a hill near Wellington. Maybe Dad meant he visited his great grandmother Lauannah or Lavinia or Laureena, whichever it was. Or maybe he was just having us on. And was John 'Farbie' May really Rosina's brother? Surely there would be some record of it in our family tree if it were true.

Joyce had mentioned the local history researcher, Lee Thurlow, several times. She said he had 'everything written up'. He kept records of Wiradjuri families, she said, and the land claim. I should go and see him if I wanted to find out more details. In the meantime, I sat down and tried to draw up Joyce's family tree to see where the gaps were and whether it crossed over with the records my father had started to research before he became ill and died more than ten years ago. I had copies of some of his notes with me and spent the evening sorting through them. Whether we had Wiradjuri ancestors or not, the mere fact of my white ancestors turning up in the Wellington Valley on the currents of English criminal and colonial policy mingled our histories inextricably.

I pictured my ancestors first setting foot on Australian soil, literally setting foot on soil I mean, not metaphorically. Perhaps because I grew up on the land, when I first set foot on the soil, in both England and Europe, there was the tear-stinging fulfilment of the imagined world meeting the actual. Each time, in fact, I knelt down, a bit pope-like, and put my hands on the ground to make sure of its earthiness. Each time a slight shock, made of faint loss and powerful joy mixed – oh God, it is just real, ordinary dirt.

I was impressed with my father's efforts at research. He was not educated past primary school and even during those short years often didn't go to class if his father needed him for harvesting or hay-making or shearing. His family were not graziers, not one of the landed gentry of Australia, but 'cockies', farmers who scratched a living from the soil. According to Dad's careful notes, my first white ancestor set foot on Australian soil at Sydney Cove on 9 October 1813, just twenty-five years after English settlement began. He was my great, great, great grandfather and his name was William Yarnold, also known as Yarnell.

William came from Worcestershire and he had just arrived on a sailing ship called the *Earl Spencer*, named after the ancestor of a well-known late-twentieth-century princess. He was short, only five feet three and a half inches tall, had black hair and hazel eyes and was described in the ship's indent as having 'dark pale' skin. He was just twenty years old – and had been convicted to a life sentence. He wasn't one of those almost innocents who 'only stole a loaf of bread', but a proper crook who stole nearly a hundred guineas from his employer, enough to live on for five years or so, the equivalent of at least $250,000 these days.

It was tempting to try to imagine the inner life of this undersized youth stepping off the gangplank one probably sunny – it was a drought – October morning. He was most likely dazzled by the light, glad to be on solid ground, relieved that he was still alive. But I can only assume what was going through his mind. Like the Wiradjuri, he left no records, no words. He probably couldn't write. I only know he was daring enough to try to radically change his life by stealing a large sum of money – and unskilled or unlucky enough to be caught.

The year he arrived the most significant thing to happen in the colony was that the Blue Mountains, 100 kilometres west of Sydney, had been crossed by Europeans for the first time. Before explaining why this mattered to William and all his descendants, a girl called Ann Smith, who wasn't even born when William stepped off the boat, needs to arrive as well.

At four feet ten and half inches, Ann was even shorter than William. She had brown hair and dark brown eyes and a 'dark ruddy' complexion. I'm not sure what William's 'dark pale' skin looked like, but I do get a picture of a rosy-cheeked Ann. She was a nurse-girl from London with no education – and according to the ship's indent, she was sent to Australia on the *Earl of Liverpool* for an apocryphal crime – stealing apples. She arrived in Sydney in April 1831. Only sixteen years old and she'd been sent to the other side of the world to a place she must have barely known existed for helping herself to a few pieces of fruit.

She was 'disposed of', as it said in the indent, to a Robert Broad of George Street, perhaps the reputed silversmith. She mustn't have been kept long, because there's a record of her marrying William Yarnold two years later, on 17 June 1833 at St John's Church in Wilberforce, a village about forty miles to the north-west of Sydney. She was eighteen years old, he was forty. I was intrigued by this short, criminal couple who found each other on the far side of the planet; they seem like a pair of well-matched delinquents, members of Britain's huge underclass, uneducated, undernourished, with no opportunities – and restless enough to do something about it.

Seventeen years after he arrived, in 1830, William had been given his ticket-of-leave, a certificate that allowed him to do paid work, set up a business and own land, but not to travel out of the district without permission. Ann was given her certificate of freedom in 1845; that's fourteen years for apples. They had a daughter, Elisabeth, the year after they married.

Why and exactly when they went to the Wellington Valley I don't know, but they were definitely there by 1849 because William was issued with a ticket-of-leave passport to travel in Wellington. It is possible he was one of the convicts sent to the Wellington Penal Colony with Percy Simpson in the 1820s and decided to return there after he was married. Or perhaps he had heard of land for free and boldly headed out into the unknown with his young wife and child.

When he was first given his ticket-of-leave, William was listed as a butcher. Twenty-one years later he is recorded only as a farmer, a landowner. Whatever his line of work, he certainly would have had dealings with the Wiradjuri. It was only thirty years since the first whites had arrived there and the Wiradjuri were still living a mainly traditional life. How they treated each other I don't know, but I'm guessing William was not an entirely reformed character. He probably took what he could get his hands on; he certainly took Wiradjuri land.

It seems Ann and William spent the rest of their lives in this valley. An Ann Smith was buried in the Pioneer Cemetery in Wellington in 1861 aged forty-five, the exact age my Ann would have been; and there's record of a William Yarnold buried in nearby Guerie. The convicts' daughter, Elisabeth, married the German immigrant, Pieter Josef Müller. Gold had been discovered in 1856 so perhaps he was a treasure-seeker. It appears Müller too did not keep a diary, but he must have decided to settle down and give his children a future as English-sounding Millers in this strange, raw place.

And that, it appears, is how the Millers of Wellington came into being. From the beginning they were farmers on Wiradjuri land, all of them descended from a pair of young crooks and a stray German who arrived in the district in the first few decades of white settlement. Perhaps they were kind to the Wiradjuri, perhaps not – they certainly dispossessed them – but whatever they did, the Millers are not in any of the history books, not even the local history ones. There are no streets or parks or creeks named after them. They were not rich or influential people, they didn't stand for office, they didn't build bridges or write books. They probably didn't even think of anything much besides looking after their families.

Except for William and Ann for whom I have an awed admiration – how could I not admire their gutsy survival of the worst the ruling class could throw at them? – I guiltily admit I've always found the rest of the Miller ancestors an unimaginative, stolid lot. I don't wish they were rich or ruled the world, I just wish they had done or said something memorable.

Perhaps that's why I like Joyce's version of the family history – it wasn't written down, but it was recounted and it was much more complex than recorded history. In her story, one of the Millers married a Wiradjuri woman, or the daughter of a Wiradjuri woman, and that has created another whole pattern of descent. Even though I was brought up to identify with an Irish, English and European tradition without a trace of Wiradjuri, and even though there is no written evidence for it, I want to believe Joyce's story because it connects me to a history on this land thousands of years beyond William and Ann's arrival 200 years ago. It would mean my DNA is made out of this place and I could imagine, however unscientifically, that there was a hidden, faded Wiradjuri part of my cells shaping something of who I am, a faintly remembered echo of blood and country.

16

Whose Native Title?

Next morning in my caravan-park cabin, I looked over the rough timeline I'd put together of the land claim. It was a sketchy record of dates of various Acts, Claims, Agreements, not comprehensive and possibly faulty. My plan was to show it to Joyce and ask her to correct the inaccuracies and fill in the details. I picked it up and took it out to the veranda to sit at the wrought-iron table.

Kookaburras and galahs were flapping about between the river gums in their noisy loutish way. I had been woken before dawn by their laughter and screeches but the sound was comforting, as the sounds of a safe childhood always are, and I'd gone back to sleep easily. I sat and watched a trail of something white, like petals, falling gently from the sky in front of me. Puzzled, I stepped off the veranda to pick one up. It was a small pink-tipped feather. In fact, the ground was scattered with them. I remembered that Wiradjuri men used to stick feathers in their hair when they were preparing for battle.

A little later I called in at my mother's unit and had morning tea with her. She was fascinated by Joyce's stories and wanted to hear all about her and the Native Title claim. Now that it was difficult for her to read, Mum spent more time watching television, keeping up with politics and current affairs and she jumped at the chance to discuss the latest issues with me. Mostly she kept her views to herself in Wellington; she knew how to keep the peace. Once, she bravely stood up at the Catholic Women's League meeting and defended single mothers, but usually she 'just banged pots and pans around loudly', as an astute friend of hers remarked, when she disagreed with the general opinion. I didn't mind telling her Joyce's stories, although I had told her most of them the evening before when I'd called in for dinner. Her beautiful sharp memory was starting to flicker on and off. I asked if I could take some of her neenish tarts to give to Joyce and when she said yes I packed them in a lunch box and left quickly.

When I presented the tarts to Joyce she popped one in her mouth immediately while I sat down at her table with my folder and cassette recorder. The room was as neat and spotless as the day before and she was as welcoming, although a little tired. She had been at the school all morning, again taking a class on Aboriginal culture.

I pulled the timeline out and showed it to her. A slightly bothered look immediately flitted across her face. She didn't want to look at my page of dates, and indeed didn't look at it the whole time I was there. I plunged in anyway.

'So who was involved in forming the Elders' Council in 1980? I've heard Teddy Bell was part of it?' I pointed at my timeline.

'They were havin' meetin's unknown to us. Teddy Bell was comin' up from Sydney. He didn't live here.' Joyce left that behind quickly, it wasn't relevant anymore, it was too long ago and too much had happened since. 'But ask Lee Thurlow if you want to know,' she added.

'Who's he again?'

'He keeps all our records. He knows all about this. You should talk to him. He knows about Rose's committee leaving us out of the claim.' She repeated then what she had told me on the phone several weeks before: that the Town Common Committee had left the Traditional Families out of the Native Title claim and included names of people who weren't even Aboriginal.

'So there's basically two sides, one lot who are descended from local Wiradjuri and the other lot who are not?'

I felt myself lining up with Joyce. It seemed obvious enough that Native Title must be established through lineage; no-one could argue with that.

'Yeah, and that's why we've put in our own claim. We've got a solicitor, a good bloke, and it's goin' to be sorted. Teitzel's 'is name.'

'When did you do that?'

'A while back.'

I doggedly decided to stay on my original track. I could ask her about the new claim later.

'Ah, let's go back to the committee who made the claim in '94. Rose Chown was the vice president and Vivienne Griffin was the president?'

'Yeah. And Rose and Vivienne are first cousins. The Bell family.'

Rose's parents were Gladys and Ronnie Bell. Gladys's mother was a Towney from Peak Hill up on the Bogan River. Ronnie's father was Roy Bell and his mother was Tillie Stanley. Vivienne's father was John, known as Jacky Bell, and he was Ronnie's brother. Her mother was Trixie Grace, and Trixie's mother was from Cowra. Teddy Bell was Vivienne's brother.

At first all this seemed to have nothing to do with the Native Title claim and who was entitled to the land; it was just family history, tangled and off the point and impossible to follow for someone outside the family. But then Joyce said something that made me realise it was the heart of the matter.

'It's passed down on the mother's side. If you are Wiradjuri or not. Granny May told us.'

Suddenly I remembered Henderson, the nineteenth-century amateur ethnologist. When he was in the Wellington Valley he had noted that the Wiradjuri traced their lineage through their mothers.

'I know, that's right,' I exclaimed. 'I've read about it. In a journal from the 1830s, Henderson, I think. That's right.'

Joyce looked at me as if I had said something completely irrelevant. I had the grace to blush. She went on. 'Granny May told us that wherever your mother's afterbirth was buried, that was your land.' She stopped and grinned. 'I said that to the Town Council when I was addressin' them and said I reckon that means I own the land down where the motel is. And they all laughed and one of 'em said, there's no doubt about ya, Joyce.'

There was that wicked grin again. *No doubt about ya.* I hadn't heard that expression for years.

So was it all to do with the mothers? Rose's mother was from the Bogan River, and Vivienne's mother was from Cowra, neither of them local Wiradjuri. Joyce's mother was born at Blacks Camp next to Nanima, so Joyce was. That part was simple enough but I had to go back over the Bell family connections to try to get it straight. As I repeated what I thought she'd said, Joyce patiently corrected me. It seemed she had family trees in her head for all the Aboriginal families in Wellington – and then I remembered that she had known who my father and grandfather and great grandmother were when she first met me, even though I'd had no idea who she was. I couldn't see how she remembered it all. I needed it written down.

It was about half an hour since I'd asked my original question about the first Native Title claim and I had gained a great deal of family history and several stories, but still didn't know how events had unfolded in Wellington.

'So when the first claim was made, were you invited to be on the committee?'

'We didn't know they were even meetin'. We didn't even know about this mediation, until another old Aboriginal fella told us we had better git along down there. This mediation. Who was it with, you know, the government fella?'

'French, was it? Robert French?' I checked my timeline. The uses of having things written down. I could see the claim was lodged in February 1994 and the newly established Native Title Tribunal headed by Justice French had held a mediation at Wellington Primary School in May the same year.

'That's 'im. French. And they were telling 'im and the papers they were the traditional owners, but they're not. They were told then they didn't have enough evidence for Native Title and they didn't get it in the end either because they're not the traditional owners. That's why we have made our own claim. The Traditional Families claim. We're called the Gallangabang Corporation. You ask Wayne Carr about it.'

'Who's he?'

'Violet Carr's 'is mum. She's on the claim, but Wayne is lookin' after it.'

'Where's he? Have you got his number?'

I wrote it down for later.

When I returned to Sydney I tried to find out why Rose's claim had failed. According to the newspapers, Justice French, who headed the mediation between all the groups, said he found the parties quite ready to negotiate behind closed doors: 'the first day was better than I'd hoped – though I can't guarantee it will lead to an agreement, I found the parties ready to talk about alternatives and not given to hardline attitudes . . . I think we have made some progress today . . .'

The same article reports Rose Chown saying she was disappointed that the claim had caused conflict within the Wiradjuri and that she was hopeful 'all parties could come to some sort of agreement'. Bill Riley, of the Wellington Aboriginal Corporation, is also reported as believing there could be a compromise. And, on the face of it, it seemed as if this optimism was justified because in February the following year an agreement was signed by all the parties, including the Wellington Lands Council, the first agreement mediated under the new Native Title Act.

But this report of a signed agreement was not the way Joyce explained it to me.

'I went along to the Annual General Meeting of the Land Council and there was a takeover by Rose's mob, which was why the agreement was signed. I was just goin' to listen and not cause any trouble.'

Then, as she recounted it, the people who were elected as office bearers in the Land Council were from 'all over the place', meaning they were not local Wiradjuri, and no-one discussed the Town Common in the open meeting.

'But then, when we all left – they told us to go – they would discuss business. The new lot discussed what was goin' to happen and passed a motion supportin' the Town Common claim.' She looked at me meaningfully.

Joyce went back to telling me about her grandfather Farbie May, and how he had organised a petition for a school at Nanima in 1908. She recounted at some length the names on the petition – Rileys, Stanleys, Daleys and Mays. I thought at first she was off on another sidetrack of family history, but she finished off with, 'And there wasn't one Bell or Ah See.' In other words, there was no record of any of Rose's or some of the other claimants' ancestors at Blacks Camp or Nanima even 100 years ago let alone 40,000 years ago. For Joyce, it was further direct evidence that some of the families who had been granted freehold ownership of the land did not have the right to it.

Joyce told me she had the petition document somewhere but we didn't get time to find it. That afternoon, however, I found a copy of it in a history book in the town library. It was just as Joyce had said. The writing was in black ink, a few blots, the signatures variations of that flowing style everyone once used. Some of the signatures with elegant loops on all the letters reminded me of my father's hand.

Back at Joyce's that same morning, I asked how Rose responded when Joyce tried to explain who was entitled to the land. Rose wouldn't listen to her evidence, Joyce said, wouldn't acknowledge her as an elder. She thought Rose felt guilty at not including all the families. It had divided the Aboriginal community.

'You used to meet people in the park and go and 'ave a cool drink and a feed in the café, it doesn't happen anymore,' she said.

The Aborigines used to hang about in Cameron Park when I was a kid. The park was their place. The bus stop for Nanima was just outside the entrance and so the park was used as a gathering place. It extended right down one side of the main shopping street, Percy Street, named after the young super-intendent of the penal colony. The park was the town's pride and joy, winning prizes in state competitions with its fine oaks and cedars and neatly tended oval and crescent-shaped beds of pansies and poppies and stocks with gravelled walkways and a playground. There was also a war memorial inscribed with the names of the fallen – including two of my great uncles, one of whom is buried in the muddy battlefield of Villiers-Bretonneux in northern France. Their names are written in gold lettering and are watched over by an angel seated on a plinth and holding a sword. Down the slope by the Bell River where the old public swimming pool used to be was a rose garden that my mother always admired. We were taken to the park to play on the swings and slippery dips, and my father took us down to the river to pee – he didn't trust public toilets – but the park clearly didn't belong to us. It belonged to the other people, the Aborigines.

Remembering the Aborigines in the park makes me wonder about belonging. I don't think it's about ownership, a relationship of law that gives the right to give or sell possessions, but, for me, belonging is about where I fit and what fits with me. It is about where I'm at one, where I'm at home. Belonging might not give any legal rights, but it is far stronger and deeper than ownership because it can't be bought or traded; in fact, I don't believe it can be destroyed by material means. If a place belongs to me, whoever owns it, it cannot be taken from me. If I belong somewhere, then it will always acknowledge me. The farm where I grew up, which my father used to own, I suddenly realise, belongs to me still; Baron Rock which no-one in my family has ever owned, has always, will always, belong to me. It must have belonged to the Wiradjuri as well, but a sense of belonging is not exclusive.

Joyce belongs in the Wellington Valley and the land belongs to her. It seems her ancestors have been in the Valley since the first Aboriginal settlers arrived unrecorded tens of thousands of years ago. But she didn't talk about that. She talked about her mother, her grandmother, her great-grandmother and her great-great-grandmother. This is what she knows, the Wiradjuri lineage of mothers. That was why, more than a decade after Rose's claim was first made, Joyce and the other fourteen families had ended up making their own Native Title claim.

'We don't want money or nothin',' Joyce clarified. 'Just our land.'

Native Title, it seems to me, is about belonging. It's about where you belong and what belongs to you. And it seems the freehold transfer of land under the Indigenous Land Use agreement is about ownership. Freehold land can be developed, built on – and, after five years, sold. When I asked Joyce what she thought was Rose's motivation for wanting ownership of the land, she looked at me and briefly rubbed her fingertips together. According to her, Rose left Wellington when she was a girl and didn't come back for twenty years. 'Twenty years is a long time. You can't just come back after twenty years.'

Joyce looked at me and I nodded, but I thought the opposite. It's not so long, you can come back, it's not so long. I had been gone for longer, nearer thirty, and the place still drew me back. Identity might fade and wear thin in the middle of the night, might flap in the wind like an old sheet, but I still belonged here. The void could lap over any time; it could soak through the flapping cotton and dissolve meaning; it was always there under my stories and would have to be faced one day, but for now, I knew this place was my ground. It wasn't a country, not a nation, but hills, valleys, creeks, dry dusty paddocks – dreamy green in a good season – gum trees, she-oaks, stony outcrops, river flats, anthills, dirt tracks, wire gates, water holes, magpies singing in the morning, kookaburras, lizards, snakes, Bathurst burrs, catheads – and over it all the wide blue dome of childhood sky. It had not proved to be a talisman against dissolution, but it felt like somewhere to stand.

17

A Wild Irishman

That evening I visited my mother. When I hugged her I felt how thin her shoulders were through the flowery cotton of her blouse. Bones. She didn't feel like eating much. On the farm we had always eaten a large 'dinner' in the middle of the day, and had 'tea' at night, which was usually left over slices of mutton and mashed potato, but now my mother literally had just a cup of tea and a piece of cake. It didn't seem enough to keep body and soul together. I poured a glass of wine and heated up my frozen Thai curry in the microwave, which my mother thought was too newfangled to use.

As I ate we watched the television news together. Afterwards, I carefully withdrew a notebook from my bag. I had a plan. I wanted to ask my mother to tell me as much of her family background as she could remember. I tried to sound nonchalant. She looked at me directly. I hadn't said *before it was too late* but she knew, there was never any fooling my mild-mannered mother, and the unspoken phrase hung uncomfortably in the air.

I've always preferred my mother's side of the family. By the time I was a teenager I had got it into my head – perhaps my mother put it there – that her side of the family was more interesting. I had the idea that they were a bit arty and brainy in a low-key sort of way; her mother's family that is, the Reidys and Kennedys, not her father's, the Whitehouses.

Mum's paternal grandfather, Abel Whitehouse, had become a fundamentalist Christian in New Zealand and her grandmother, Elanora Isbister, had left him and her young children, including Jack who became Mum's father, and gone to Australia. When he turned seventeen, young Jack followed his mother to Sydney and bore her no ill will for leaving him as a child, saying, according to Mum, 'no-one could live with the bloody old man'. Jack became a house-painter and an accompanist at the silent movies and, said my mother, played the sweetest trumpet anyone ever heard. He was a man of sharp wit and thoughtful politics who couldn't stand small-mindedness and gossip – and he was an alcoholic. My mother adored her father and modelled herself on him, except that she has never touched alcohol. I never met Jack as he died the year I was born. He came late to the town, arriving around 1920, and by then the Wiradjuri origins of various families had already been forgotten, at least by the whites.

The Kennedy–Reidy family he married into had arrived much earlier from Ireland. The Kennedys were from Queens County and the Reidys from Limerick. There were also O'Meara and Quain ancestors – among thousands of Irish immigrants arriving in Wellington and the central west in the mid nineteenth century. As far as I know, Patrick Reidy was my first Irish ancestor to arrive in the Wellington Valley.

He named his property on the banks of Curra Creek Sarsfield after the renowned Limerick rebel leader, one of thousands of names of European heroes and beloved home towns transplanted to Australia. He buried his infant son on the bank of Curra Creek in 1850 and some years later donated this land to the Catholic Church for a cemetery. Today there is a whole tribe of Reidys buried there as well as my father. I don't look at his headstone because when she ordered it, my mother asked the stonemason to leave a space for her name on it. I don't want to see the blank that will have to be filled one day.

I thought of Patrick as 'a wild Irishman' because the only story I had about him was that he raced his horse along the bed of Curra Creek in front of a roaring flood. It wasn't a story my mother told me, but one I found in an odd little photocopied history of land ownership in the Wellington district. I imagined him galloping recklessly along the sandy bed of the creek, simply for the hell of it, the brown water rushing and swirling behind his horse's hooves. Patrick must have remained a lover of his own homeland, not just because he named his property after an Irish independence leader, but because on his tombstone, beautifully carved with threaded shamrocks, are the words *Native of Co. Limerick*, which suggests that his birthplace was the truest thing about him.

More than a hundred years after Patrick, my sisters and brothers and I were brought up 'Australian', but under my mother's guidance, having a stronger identification with the Irish rather than the English or long-ago Germans of our father's side. It was a class loyalty as well – the English were more likely to be toffs. The Kennedys and Reidys were proud, however, of the fact that all their ancestors had freely chosen to come to Australia; none of them were convicts. By the time of my grandmother's generation they were respectable publicans and would have been reasonably well off, my mother said, if John Reidy hadn't had a heart attack and died after defending someone in a scuffle outside the pub.

My grandmother, Linda Reidy, and her five sisters and pregnant mother had to survive on their own in genteel poverty, doing sewing, giving piano lessons and teaching at the local convent. According to my mother they loved literature, playing and listening to music, having political discussions and generally living a life of the mind, and so they gained in my mind the status of intellectuals and artists, or at least as good a claim as my family could make to that territory.

I couldn't find any Wiradjuri connections to my mother's side of the family. The Irish ancestors were, it appeared, simply part of the infinite patterning of chance that created this ordinary country town in the middle of another people's homeland. In the strange way the world works, months after the conversation with my mother that night, I found out that it was, in fact, Patrick Reidy who connected me most directly to the Native Title claim.

Since I had aligned myself with the Reidys and Kennedys, while I was living in Paris it was natural to travel to Ireland. I set out with Anthony, wondering whether there would be any sense of recognition, any sense of homecoming. I don't think memory and history can be genetically coded, although neuro-physiological research has revealed long-term memory is chemically stored in our cells, so perhaps it was not so far-fetched to think such complex chemistry could stain and colour genes. Perhaps I had inherited an Irish sensibility.

We flew in from Paris, and after staying a few nights in Dublin, drove down through the middle of Ireland, around the Ring of Kerry and then up to Limerick. It was June, the beginning of summer, and everywhere, just as I had been taught to imagine, there were the emerald fields dotted with castles and abbeys and stony villages held close under damp grey skies.

It was also the time of the local council elections and on every oak, yew and chestnut tree – and almost every electricity pole and fence post – there were election posters bearing the candidates' names and portraits. Oddly, in this foreign country, all the names were familiar. It was like driving through a list of names from my childhood: Reidy and Kennedy, of course, and Agnew, Burke, Brennan, Daley, Devine, Ryan, O'Brien, O'Rourke, Hughes, Knowles, Kelly, Keeley, Lynch, Munn, McCarthy, Nolan, Knuckey, Sheridan, Spargo, Shannon, Quirk, Quain – almost every name echoed in a Wellington family, the familiar chant repeating for hundreds of miles. I had not realised how many of the town's families had originally come from Ireland, had not even thought about it before, but it made me curious to know why so many had left this romantic green place for a dry wilderness. The first time I went back to Wellington afterwards, I visited the cemetery with my mother and it didn't take much comparing of the earliest dates of Irish names to realise most of them must have come out during or just after the Great Potato Famine of 1845.

Anthony and I drove on, drinking in the romantic dream

of the auld country. In the churches and abbeys and Celtic crosses it was easy to see the controlling story of religion, but stronger than that, more influential it struck me, was the landscape itself; the rocky outcrops, the cliffs, the wild high stony places, even after thousands of years of settlement didn't seem tamed. This must have been what Patrick Reidy yearned for under the hot sky of Australia.

Finally, we drove over the county border into Limerick and parked by the side of the road. I waited for the damp green country to speak to me. I got out of the car and walked through the sodden grass on the verge to lean on a stone wall and breathe in the coolness. My boots were already darkened with wet, the fine misty air moistened my hair and cheeks. It felt fresh and welcoming.

'It suits you, this climate,' Anthony said.

'I always knew it would.'

There was a derelict stone cottage by the side of the road, roof tiles broken, windows gone. It was a bleak little house, isolated in a bleak flat landscape along what would have been a muddy lane. There were no trees and no evidence of there ever having been a garden, no stone wall to give the cottage any kind of distinction. I thought of the cold and the poverty and grey skies and the lack of food and education. I got back in the car and we drove along the cold-looking inlet towards the city of Limerick, but as we skirted around the suburban edges I decided not to stay. I might have looked at home but it didn't feel like my place after all.

I had inherited Irish red hair from my ancestors, and an Irish love of words and storytelling, but the landscape did not know me. If I stayed longer I might have begun to see through the drizzle and over the emerald fields and it might recognise me, but as it was, I was an outsider. This place was the home of my ancestors, not mine.

I thought of Patrick Reidy lying in the cemetery under the dry grass at Wellington and wondered if he ever felt at home in the hot harsh country he had ended up in. I come from transplanted people, I suddenly realised. It might mean we always grow a little crooked and ill at ease.

18

Gold

I had been in Wellington for several days, talking to Joyce and seeing my mother, and was ready to return to the city. Despite the fresh morning air an odd desolateness had crept up on me, the return of a feeling of being caught there, the base note of my teenage years. There was only a morning to spend in the local library – which was now housed in the old bowling club – and then I could leave.

I knew that after the missionaries and farmers had arrived, gold was found near Wellington and I wondered how its discovery had affected the Wiradjuri and my ancestors. There was no record of either my convict or Irish ancestors rushing to search for gold in Wellington, although Gran Miller's father was a gold-panner on the Bathurst goldfields along the Turon River. Perhaps they had already had enough excitement coming from the other side of the world and were happy to supply the food to the hundreds of people who began flooding into Wellington and nearby villages of

Bodangara and Iron Bark, where gold seams had been found in the 1850s.

When I told him about my search, the librarian plied me with local history books and articles and promised to send me more. I settled down at one of the desks with the light streaming in and began with an illustrated history of the search for gold.

As I had imagined, the goldfields were often quite violent places. There were a number of accounts of bushrangers' attacks around Wellington; a particularly tragic one happened on the goldfields in 1863 when two masked men held up Mr John Lake's store in broad daylight. As Mr Lake rushed forward to stop them he trod on and killed his own sleeping baby son. I thought of Mr Lake, and then, Mrs Lake, how neither of them would ever have been able to forget the image of a heavy boot coming down on a tiny, beloved body. When I read this account, history disappeared and the pain was here in the present, 150 years after it happened.

Some of the bushranging attacks occurred even before the gold rush; one at Bushrangers Creek, which obviously earned it its name. When I was a child, Bushrangers Creek Road was the 'other' way home to the farm. Instead of turning left at the Showground – once owned by Patrick Reidy – occasionally my father would drive straight ahead and there would be a buzz in the car; we were going Bushrangers Creek way! Even such a small deviation from the usual was something to be relished.

The dirt road went up through the bush-covered hills, past a collection of tin shacks, which I later learned was the remains of an Aboriginal settlement, past the turn-off to

Mount Arthur, which had a panoramic view of the town, and past the old town reservoir surrounded by desolate scrub. This road was more lonely and strange altogether, less comforting but more thrilling. The uninhabited hills felt like they didn't want anyone living there and they seemed to only reluctantly allow anyone to even drive through. When the bush finally cleared into the rolling paddocks there was a sense of relief that we had got through safely once again. Something dreadful could easily happen Bushrangers Creek way and yet it was the way we longed to go.

What happened there was not so dreadful. Two bushrangers, Jacky-Jacky and Redcap, whose names suggest they were Aboriginal, had escaped from Bathurst jail. They were going to kill a Mr Piggins, but he hid among his cattle while the bushrangers walked into his house where his wife had just given birth. They decently left, unaware that the resourceful Mrs Piggins had £200 hidden under her birthing pillow. Several days later, the outlaws were captured at Bushrangers Creek – but not before Redcap had fired a shot at Sergeant Sheedy, taking off his whiskers and grazing his jaw. Though it matters little now, and although Mr Piggins's actions resulted in his child living and Mr Lake's in his child dying, I could not help feeling disdain for Mr Piggins crouching among the cows, and a painful, desperate admiration for Mr Lake, who could never rest again.

During the gold rush the Chinese first arrived in Wellington. Many arrived after the 1861 anti-Chinese riots on the goldfields at Lambing Flat and set up camp along gold-bearing rivers and creeks. Hundreds worked the alluvial deposits along Mookerawa Creek and built a mile-long water race out of stone, which was much admired and envied. The Celestials, as they were called, lived in tents on the goldfields and in town at the bottom of Ward Street where they had opium dens, strange-smelling herbs, paper lanterns and 'berry-brown' children. In Ward Street now there is the town swimming pool and a few ordinary houses, nothing that hints at an exotic past.

While Europeans worked individually, many of the Chinese gold seekers worked in large extended family groups, apparently more similar to Wiradjuri than colonial society. Still, others were coolies working for 'mandarins' who wore red sashes and rode around on horses strictly supervising the workers. In the evenings the coolies gambled, smoked opium and drank sujo. The local history books say that because they worked harder than Europeans and found gold where others didn't, and they kept to themselves and sent their gold home to China, there was jealousy and ill-feeling towards them. But it seems the Chinese did not keep entirely to themselves, or at least later on they mixed more, because there are Aboriginal–Chinese in Wellington. I remember the Ah Sees and Loosicks; I saw them around town, but I didn't know them. Even in a small town there weren't a lot of reasons to cross fine degrees of social difference.

After leaving the library I called in on my mother for a quick goodbye. She began reminiscing about the Chinese in her childhood, market gardeners and shop owners. In the 1920s she started school with a Chinese boy, Henry Ling, who later owned a stock and station store in Wellington and who now lived in one of the retirement units across from her.

Her family shopped at Fong Lee's general store in Percy Street during the Depression because they were the only shopkeepers who let people buy food supplies 'on tick' for months at a time. She recalled, too, the Chinese gardeners carrying their vegetables for sale up from the river in swinging baskets carried on a pole across their shoulders. She reminded me there was a display of Chinese memorabilia in the History Museum, but it would have to wait until next visit.

Until recently, I hadn't thought the Chinese history in Wellington had anything to do with me. But a couple of years ago, a cousin of mine had an eye operation. This would seem irrelevant except that the surgeon remarked on her Mongolian fold, an eyelid construction, which, he said, only appeared in people of Asian descent. This particular cousin is a double-cousin, we share the same four grandparents, which means we have identical genealogies. Here was another mystery in the family background, an unarguable strand of genes from an Asian ancestor. It made me think again about Joyce's story – our shared Wiradjuri ancestors. It is clear that what is written down is not the whole story.

19

Native Title Fight

Back in Kings Cross after the trip west, the seasons had changed. The leaves of the plane trees in the street had turned brown and started to fall; the rustling sounds and bare branches and the accents of backpackers returning from their summer of exploring gave the neighbourhood a foreign tang. The cooler air was crisp and I felt the gentle surge of nostalgia that flows into me every autumn; the odd yearning for another time and place. It was melancholic but strangely reassuring, as if I was connecting to past cycles. The smells of damp leaves and wet bark were familiar although they were never part of my childhood – as if I was remembering a European childhood of coolness and mists that I never had.

I arranged to meet Gaynor, the anthropologist who had been the advisor for Rose's original claim. She arrived at my place with a video documentary that had been produced about ten years before when that first Native Title claim was made. We chatted while I made a cup of tea. She had come to Australia as a young woman and had fallen in love with the bush from the very first time she had walked out into it. I've come across that 'love at first sight' before: people who arrive here as adults and it's as if the Australian landscape was what they had been waiting for all their lives, its ancient dry spirit capturing them instantly.

I have often wondered whether I would have fallen in love with it if I had not grown up in this landscape, or whether I would have only seen it as harsh and bedraggled, lacking all grace and charm, as the early English settlers did. I suspect that my head full of a European mythology of beauty would have prevented me from seeing or feeling the mystical presence that saturates the bush. After all, I fell in love with Europe in an instant – what sort of faithfulness is that?

And what am I really saying when I use words like *ancient dry spirit* and *mystical presence*? Is there a sub-atomic vibration in the land and the vegetation here that is different from the vibration of Europe or anywhere else? A chemistry of being? A physics? Is there something in the apricot-coloured trunk of an apple gum, the rough bark of a she-oak, the grey-green eucalypt leaves, the fine dust under the kurrajong, the sand in the creek bed, the rocky slope above the river, the kangaroo grass on the hill, the red earth itself? Something that persistently and silently promises revelation. I don't know. But I acknowledge something unmistakeable happens in the bush that I cannot help being aware of and which I have not felt anywhere else, an inexplicable sense of the landscape dreaming itself into being. As much as the beauty of Europe enchants – a spell made of childhood reading, of meadows and hazelwoods and ruined chateaux – it has never promised revelation.

I watched the documentary with Gaynor. The camera panned over the familiar landscape of low hills and river flats, a landscape I knew as well as the faces and bodies of my family. I felt the pleasure of seeing my place, myself, reflected. Here it was on the television screen. It must be real. It must matter.

One of the elders at Nanima, Jim Stanley, said, 'For a young girl to come along and do this to the old people . . .' and then was lost for words.

He was talking about Rose, a woman who would have been at least forty at that stage. His voice was not at all angry, just saddened and shocked. His look of bewilderment and hurt reminded me of someone. I realised it was the same look my father had on his face when, with the education he had provided, I dismissed what he believed in.

Rose, sitting in the open air with her committee, at ease with the camera, engaging and commanding at the same time, said, 'These people who say they are elders . . . I really don't know, there was no need to consult with the people of Nanima. These people want to run it for their own gain.'

The interviewer suggested Rose might be accused of the same thing and she laughed and said, no, she was doing it for all the people to have a future. She had long, thick black hair, a broad face, a large build, that loose-limbed way of sitting and standing and walking. In one shot, she sat leaning forward, legs apart, laughing easily, but there was something edgy in her manner. Her eyes were ready to make an accusation or defend against one. I had the immediate impression that I would rather she was on my side than against me. I remembered how quickly she had taken control of the first telephone call and knew that I hadn't stood a chance.

The families on Rose's committee were Ah See, Amatto, Bell, Peachy and Towney. There were other claimants represented, but these families each had members on the committee. Joyce's group of claimants didn't exist as a legal entity at the time of the documentary, but the families associated with it stood there in a loose group – Rileys, Carrs and Stanleys.

After we watched the video, Gaynor expanded on the documentary. She agreed that part of the conflict lay in the fact that the NSW Aboriginal Land Rights Act decreed membership of local Land Councils was to be based on residency rather than tribal identity. This meant that whether you were Wiradjuri or not, you could still sit on the local Land Council. She said that at first Rose didn't want the Land Council to have anything to do with the claim, but then saw it would be to her advantage to have it onside and so she organised for people from her group to be elected onto it, which backed up what Joyce had told me.

'Rose's mob systematically took over key positions in key organisations, even the Health Co-op that Joyce had devoted years of her life to setting up.'

I commented, knowledgeably I thought, that Wiradjuri identity came through the mothers so Rose had no right to local land.

'That's not true. I suppose Joyce told you that.'

'Yes, but not just Joyce. I found it in my research as well. An early ethnologist, Henderson, I think, he said so as well. You're Wiradjuri if your mother is.'

'Wiradjuri is a language group. There's a blurring of concepts here. And Aboriginal identity is not just through biological family, it's a whole pattern of elements. Your totem comes through your mother. In relation to the land, it's also about who has the right to identify with country and who has the right to speak for it – not the same thing either.'

'So how is someone Wiradjuri then?'

'We need to go back a bit. Traditionally, the moiety of Wiradjuri was matrilineal. Moiety is the division of a clan in the same language group into skin groups and determines kinship,' Gaynor explained. It was her area of research, she had written a number of papers and a couple of books on Wiradjuri history. 'It means you can have skin sisters, brothers, cousins, aunts and uncles that you are not biologically related to. The skin group dictates all social relations including who can marry whom, and who must avoid whom. It's ritually significant and determines what your totem will be. Most of the Wiradjuri were one of two totems, the crow and the eagle-hawk. Your moiety gives you the right to identify spiritually with certain areas of land, but so does where you were born, who your mother and father are. Couples always lived in the woman's country and your moiety and therefore totem was passed down through your mother.'

'What about now? Do Wiradjuri still know their moiety or totem?'

'No, they don't, not any of the people I've talked to, but there is still the notion of the right to identify with country and the right to speak for it. You can identify with country, have a spiritual right to it, but you don't necessarily have the right to speak for it. And that's distinct from ritual or economic or political rights as well.'

'What gives you the right to identify with country?'

'You can have it through your mother or father or where you grew up.'

'Doesn't that mean Rose has the right to identify?'

I was thinking of myself, plaintively. Don't I have the right?

'Rose left Wellington as a teenager and didn't come back for twenty years. She still has the right to identify, but not the right to speak for country. She did not try to reconnect with the elders and reintegrate herself. She spoke as a resident with a childhood connection, but in Aboriginal culture, that does not give the right to speak. This is the heart of the problem, the real offence. The Land Rights Act, in effect, collapsed the distinction between the right to identify and the right to speak for country, but for Aboriginal people it is still law. Under Aboriginal law, Rose had no right to speak for country.'

I immediately thought of the look in Jim Stanley's eyes and the tone of his voice. He could not comprehend how Rose could give such offence – *For a young girl to come along and do this to the old people*. It's all there in the phrasing: *a young girl* – she wasn't an elder and had no right; *to come along* – she came from somewhere else; *do this to the old people* – they had not been accorded the respect they were due.

Afterwards I realised that was what Joyce had been trying to tell me. Recounting family lineage was not to tell me who was related to whom; she was speaking about Aboriginal law and tradition, about who was entitled to speak for country. I had not properly listened, because I had already decided Aboriginal culture didn't exist anymore in Wellington. And it is true that there isn't much traditional Aboriginal culture these days – at least not observably. All the Aborigines in Wellington and Nanima live in houses, go to school, go to the pub, play football, shop at Bi-Lo, same as the whites. The older women wear the same unobtrusive style of skirt and cardigan as my mother, the young men the same baseball caps and t-shirts as my sons. It's the stories of family and kinship and identity that are different.

20

Native Title Histories

I couldn't help feeling that what I had been told so far might be unfair to Rose. She had been struggling for the Town Common land for fourteen years. She obviously felt she belonged in Wellington too. There must be more to her story. But before I begged Rose for an interview again, I had to clarify the sequence of events. I had the timeline, but I needed to try to fill in the factual gaps that Joyce had partly woven over with stories. Not being a historian with a proper dedication to facts, there was a strong temptation to spread out what I had and smudge the edges of each bit to cover the blank space.

The central aspect that needed to be clear, even before the timeline, was the Native Title process itself. I sat down with the National Native Title Tribunal's guidelines: first, a group of people, claimants, must form themselves into a legally recognisable body, then lodge an application with the Federal Court. At the same time, a separate body, the Native Title

Tribunal, which has no power to determine claims, must decide whether the claim can be registered.

Registration is the key, because once a claim is registered, the claimants have certain rights, such as the right to negotiate over use of the land. This right is given even before the legitimacy of the claim is determined, so the tribunal has to be sure it's a reasonable claim. In a sense, registration is an acknowledgement of Native Title. Practically, it is treated as an acknowledgement and gaining registration is celebrated as a victory – the claimants have shown beyond reasonable doubt that the land is rightfully theirs.

Because of the rights registration gives, the tribunal must establish that the people on the claim can be clearly identified, and that there has been a continuing physical connection with the land. But a physical connection can be a slippery thing to prove, especially when, as with the Wellington Wiradjuri, the traditional way of life – hunting and gathering – has not been possible for a long time. This means there has to be an investigation of the claimants' family trees and life histories, and so anthropologists, like Gaynor, are often called in to gather evidence. The tribunal publicises the claim so that anyone – pastoralists, local councils, mining companies or other Aborigines – can object. If there are objections or interests, the Federal Court makes orders about mediation and the tribunal organises the mediations.

Now all this can take a few years and if the tribunal decides the claim can be registered then the case goes ahead in the court. If everyone is in agreement a determination is simply made, but if not, then a trial follows where the evidence of all sides is heard.

This is the framework for what was happening in Wellington, an elaborate, wiry construction of law, mostly invisible to most of the people involved, determining the validity of their every move. Joyce and Rose both recounted stories about their ancestors to anyone who asked – lawyers, anthropologists, journalists – trying to make their words affect this strange legal machinery, trying to make it yield by its own arcane magic the right to 183 hectares of land.

So what had happened in Wellington? As far as I have been able to piece it together in my own haphazard fashion, this is more or less what unfolded.

After the mediation presided over by Robert French in 1994, the New South Wales government had to sign the agreement before it could be lodged with the tribunal. The then Liberal government wasn't over-eager to sign. A newspaper report records that the claimant's lawyer, Mr Paul Coe, himself Wiradjuri, said, 'the New South Wales government is being its usual racial and discriminatory self'. But the incoming Labor government was just as reluctant. It stated it had no desire to block the claim but expressed reservations about the level of evidence of ongoing connection with the land.

There was legal opinion that the lack of a 'threshold of evidence' of connection meant any Native Title claim, no matter how vexatious or implausible, could be registered by the tribunal. Theoretically, any Aboriginal person could make a claim over any Crown land, which if registered, meant the claimant could intervene in its use. It's pretty clear that no-one in government wanted to open that can of worms, so no-one was going to do anything until a threshold was set. The claim stayed on ministers' desks as months turned into years.

After the claim stalled I couldn't find any more clues until the September 1997 Native Title newsletter, which said the claim was due back in the Federal Court. Here it was noted for the first time that a new solution might be possible: a freehold transfer of the land via an Indigenous land use agreement.

The following year, Gaynor withdrew as anthropological consultant because, in her judgment, there wasn't enough evidence to support the claim. She wrote to Rose and told her she could no longer work with her. Rose and her committee asked that the case be referred to the Federal Court. The *Sydney Morning Herald* again reported that the Wellington Common was 'close to being handed back to the Aborigines'.

It must have been feeling like groundhog day for Rose. She was quoted as saying: 'Young people have grown big and gone the wrong way and some elders have died in the years we have waited for politicians to come to a decision.' It was such a rhythmic poetic sentence; if that was actually the way she talked, I had to meet her.

In 1999 the Aboriginal Affairs minister in the New South Wales government, Dr Andrew Refshauge, appointed a mediator, Tim Moore, to negotiate an Indigenous land use agreement. Mr Moore was optimistic, saying it would only be four or five months before land could be given to the claimants. By then the claimants had agreed that any Native Title claims would be surrendered for freehold title. It wasn't much to surrender; their Native Title claim had failed because the conditions required for the identity of claimants had not been met.

In the meantime, Rose had tired of all the to-and-fro and moved into an old tin hut on the Common where her grandmother Matilda Bell had lived. She said, again so poetically, 'Old government rigmarole takes such a long time.' She was directed to change her list of claimants to include those Wiradjuri not presently living in the area, and excluding those not eligible. I could hear Joyce saying, 'see, exactly, they're not entitled'. But after being excluded for so long, after not being considered and respected as elders, there was no way Joyce and her 'Traditional Families', as she called them, were going to join in.

It was Rose the media wrote lyrically about when the July 2000 announcement was, at last, made:

'It's a beautiful evening,' said Mrs Chown, as rain fell on the tin roof of her grandmother's humpie. She had received the news that the hand-written application she lodged in January 1994, just 17 days after the Act was passed, had finally led the Government to announce that the Wiradjuri would own the land.

It was sounding like a great conclusion for Rose. Mr Moore said it looked like the land would be formally handed over by the end of the year, but it was still going on by mid 2002, when the claim was finally lodged. By then one objection had also been lodged – from Joyce's mob. On and on it went, but the official records continued to sound as if everything was unfolding as neatly as it should.

Hansard records Refshauge saying:

This agreement marks a significant outcome for the people of Wellington . . . It will resolve the oldest native title claim lodged in Australia. I am sure that *the spirit of co-operation that has led to this agreement will serve as a model for future agreements between Indigenous and non-Indigenous people in New South Wales.* (my italics)

How straightforward and convincing the written, official version is, so reassuring and unified. Anyone reading the records – including the parliamentary ones – could be forgiven for thinking the whole Native Title process for the Wellington Wiradjuri was simple and no-one had ever disagreed with anyone. No bitter conflict within the Aboriginal community, no accusations or insinuations, no hurt, no split.

In following the story of the Wiradjuri, I have had to face the fact that, even knowing how questionable reality is, how it can dissolve overnight, part of me still wants to believe in a smooth, coherent, continuous story. It is an attitude easily exploited by those who have reasons to hide the complex truth. I had begun to see that the remembered version, Joyce's version – many-stranded, tangled, subjective – might be more truthful. History, by definition written, is not necessarily the truth.

21

Patrick Reidy and the Wiradjuri

It was late autumn, months since my first failed phone call to Rose. Outside the air was cool and leaves swirled and gathered under parked cars and flattened themselves onto windscreens. I curled up with local history books sent to me from the Wellington Library. There were still gaps in the Native Title conflict, but I wanted to find out what happened in the 150 years between the missionaries' zealous efforts to save Native souls in the early nineteenth century and the crime statistics of the late twentieth.

Like my own ancestors, the Wiradjuri didn't write anything down. And neither did white observers write much after the initial exotic difference of the Natives wore off. Perhaps the eighteenth-century urge to observe and record had finally given way to the nineteenth-century desire for exploitation and progress. Perhaps the Natives had become Abos and were simply a nuisance in the great surge of development. Whichever it was, I found myself missing the obsessive recording of the missionaries.

There were still some threads I could follow: the few local history books and Lee Thurlow, the local historian whom Joyce had mentioned. I could talk to Joyce again and to one of her friends, Evelyn, who still lived out at Nanima.

The earliest history was written in 1906 by the editor of the local newspaper, who mentioned only that 'the Blacks' soon thinned out and that in 1840 sixty troopers were stationed across the river at Montefiores where a village had begun to grow, to 'quell disturbances by blacks on outer stations'. He says, sympathetically, that they naturally objected to their land being taken by unscrupulous white men.

A later history reports that an Aborigine from Wellington had originally shown Lieutenant Percy Simpson the route from Bathurst and then there is no further mention of Aborigines for the next 125 years of the town's history. It's one of those smooth, glossy accounts written to celebrate the town and its families, padded out with advertisements for various shops and businesses. I couldn't help checking the chapter titled 'Men and Women Who Played Their Part in the Work of the Town' to see if any of my ancestors were mentioned. I was foolishly pleased to see five Reidys and one Kennedy listed and wanted to immediately check each entry.

I skimmed down the page with Patrick Reidy's name on it. The words jumped out at me. In 1867 a committee of three men was appointed to look into how and where to set up a Town Common. The committee settled on a fine parcel of land along the Macquarie River a few miles south-east of the town and that year the Common was formally gazetted. Although the men on the committee probably didn't see it that way, this was the moment the land was officially taken from the Wiradjuri. One of the three men on that committee of land thieves was my own ancestor, Patrick Reidy!

I stared at the entry. I could hardly believe it. It wasn't just symbolic to say my ancestors took the land from the Wiradjuri in the first place. After all this time I had discovered one of them, Patrick Reidy, really did take it.

As Patrick's bones lie in the soil by Curra Creek, he can't be called to account for anything anymore. In his day I suppose he strode about, bearded and waist-coated, once a poor, rebel Limerickman, now lord of his domain at last. I am sure he didn't think of himself as a land thief. To him, this land was freely available for the taking. There were no fences or stone walls or deeds of title – and the Natives didn't seem to be doing anything with it. He could not have had any idea of the effect of the loss of land on the people who had lived on it forever, any idea that their descendants would be sticking needles in their arms, or that his own descendants would be mugged in the streets because of it.

In the most recent history, Patrick was mentioned again, this time in connection with an Aboriginal cricket team formed in 1882. They soon 'displayed a mastery of the game which embarrassed other players'. The cricket field they used was at Sarsfield, Patrick's farm on the banks of the Curra Creek. I pictured him again, still bearded, but this time in cream flannels, watching the elegant swing of willow in skilful black hands. Perhaps he had started to get ideas about himself by now, imitating his former English lords with his own wooded park and cricket meadow.

The following year, the story continued, the local Aboriginal cricket team beat the Wellington eleven by twenty-eight runs in the first innings and the white team declined to finish the match. Shortly afterwards a return match was organised and once more the Aboriginal team beat the white men, this time by five runs. The local paper said, with a curious pride: 'The dusky sons of the soil marched off triumphantly victorious, quite prepared to beat the English eleven players should they come this way.'

Lester Daley, the Aboriginal kid who sat in the desk behind me in high school, played cricket. I remember his white shirt untucked, revealing dark skin above his white shorts. He played in the same team as my brother Terry and they often won. But it was for rugby league football that Aborigines became stars in Wellington – and across the country. I wondered why they didn't keep playing cricket. Perhaps the white teams got tired of being beaten and wouldn't play them anymore.

The next mention of Aborigines was the 1901 Census, which recorded there were sixty-eight Aborigines in the Wellington district. This seems a ridiculously low number, since 100 years later there was more than 1000, but in those days, only 'full-bloods' were counted as Aborigines: 'Oh but they are half white, you can't count them as Aborigines.' Of course they were counted as Aborigines when it came to applying for jobs or being allowed to vote or own property or being approved of as suitable marriage partners for people like my grandmother.

The final mention is just a few years later. The Sanitary Inspector reported to the Wellington Council on the condition of the Aborigines' camp near the Town Common where there were eighteen huts sheltering up to eighty people. This was Blacks Camp where Joyce's mother, Maggie May, was born. 'Upon enquiry,' said the Inspector, 'I was informed that as many as 13 people were living in a small three-roomed hut.' Aborigines had lung illnesses and some had died of tuberculosis. There were no sanitary facilities and there was a serious risk that the town's water supply would be contaminated.

This last comment seemed to have been the motivation for a demand that the camp be moved. It echoed the story Bill Riley and Joyce told of their grandfather writing a letter to Queen Victoria about the flooding and poor conditions, and her letter in reply advising them to relocate. Whatever the motivating force, council or queen, they were moved to the present Nanima site in 1910. The Aboriginal Welfare Board built some houses, which the local newspaper reported were little better than the huts they had left.

There was nothing more to be found in the local history books. For my own ancestors, Patrick, land thief and cricketer, and a handful of others were named. The Wiradjuri were barely recorded as a people and not one individual was mentioned. Not a single name.

But the Wiradjuri were there, working as stockmen, drovers, fencers, shearers, shed-hands, scrub-cutters, horse-breakers, shepherds and general farmhands – all the wide range of skilled work necessary on country properties. According to Gaynor's research, once the supply of convicts dried up, workers were needed to replace them, and once their hunting land was taken, the Aborigines needed work. In the 1880s, over eighty per cent of Aborigines in Wellington were employed. They sometimes stayed on one property but more often moved onto another district when seasonal work was finished. In those days without large machinery, farm work required a lot of men so not even small 'cockies' could run a property on their own. This means that my early ancestors, the Kennedys and Reidys and Müllers, and even the ex-convict William Yarnold, once he became a land-owner, must have had Aboriginal workers.

The Wiradjuri women around Wellington, like Joyce, also worked on the larger properties as maids and cooks and nurse-maids and sometimes as wet nurses and midwives. They were mostly younger women who, if they liked their employers, stayed until they were married and then followed their hus-bands' work. Because the women were often involved with the care and bringing up of children, they were also taught English social skills and etiquette.

The Aboriginal men had better relations with their employ-ers than women did. They said they would yarn together with the boss at smoko and the boss might lend his truck for the weekend – whereas Aboriginal women said the wives were 'all la-de-da'. It was because the bosses nearly always worked alongside their Aboriginal hands, doing the same hard physi-cal work, whereas the wives 'didn't actually work with you, they told you what to do and told you to do it again if you didn't do it properly'.

What else did the Wellington Wiradjuri do for 150 years?

They were born at Blacks Camp or Nanima and deliv-ered by Maggie May; attended Nanima school; a handful went on the bus to high school; some attended church until it blew away in the big storm; tried to avoid hospital when they were sick; played sport exceptionally well; swam and fished in the Macquarie River; met for corroborees up until the 1870s; occasionally looked for bush food; cooked and cleaned and sewed for whites; dressed up and went to dances; drank beer when the palest of them could buy it; sang, played guitar; rode horses and sulkies; visited Aunties and Uncles; married – sometimes other Wiradjuri, sometimes whites or Chinese; argued with each other; fought in wars – the Boer, the First and Second World Wars; endured removal of children, discriminatory laws and racist attitudes; sat on verandas and talked, cried quietly, and laughed out loud in that loose, immoderate way that used to scare me a bit as a child when I walked past them hanging about Cameron Park. By that time, the time of my conscious childhood, the last corroboree was over by nearly 100 years, moieties were forgotten, the beautiful bora trees were burned and the Wiradjuri kept to themselves. They were like shadows in their own place, on the edge of life, or at least that was how I thought of them until I found a photograph taken in the 1950s of a Wiradjuri couple outside a tin hut in the market gardens.

The photograph showed a handsome man, Gindin, in an open-necked shirt, sportscoat and felt hat, standing in a 'cool' fifties pose – arms loosely held in front of him, beer in one hand, one leg bent as if he's about to dance. Mona, a pretty woman in a swing skirt, is hanging off his elbow. The way they are standing says so much about them and their relationship to each other – he is the centre around which she revolves – but also their relaxed relationship to their surroundings. They are at home, confident, stylish.

Gindin in particular, is conscious of how he presents. He reminded me of Kabbarrin in the missionary journals when he refused to wear the blue coat Watson had bought because it made him look like a 'new chum'. Gindin would have disdained the blue coat as well. He might be living in a tin hut, but he's never going to be less than stylish. It's a consciousness of appearance that connects him as much to Paris as to Kabbarrin – it's the look that matters. Gindin and Mona both look so at ease, so in charge of their world. Their elegance suggests that life wasn't all bad during those years for the Wiradjuri, but it's not just their awareness of self and style that intrigued. Their stance, their gaze, made me realise, that, for them, we were the shadows, irrelevant white folk on the fringe of their lives.

22

The Town Historian

By late winter, I was heading west to Wiradjuri country again. This time the hillsides and paddocks were smoothly green under a bleached feathery cloak of late winter grasses, a luxury for this country. The barren drought of my childhood, greyish brown and disheartening, had repeated monotonously since then. Some seasons were good but growing anything was always a struggle. For the Wiradjuri, even before the Europeans arrived, cyclic seasons of severe drought must have made finding enough food and game difficult at times.

I had arranged another meeting with Joyce and her friend Evelyn, who had lived out at Nanima for years. Before that though, I was going to meet Lee Thurlow. He was reputed to know more about this town's story than everyone else put together. I hadn't forgotten my hasty promise to Joyce about finding the bora ground. If anyone knew where it was, it would be Lee.

★

He was waiting for me on his veranda when I pulled up outside his small weatherboard house. I approached his front gate with my papers and recorder, conscious of looking like a city interloper. He was in his mid forties, with an intense, alert, slightly 'ready for attack' manner and the kind of wiry energy that never sits still. Because Joyce had said he knew all about Wiradjuri families I'd been expecting him to be Aboriginal and so was surprised that he looked white. He said later he had as much, or rather, as little, Aboriginal background as I did; an Indigenous ancestor back in the mid nineteenth century.

We stood on the veranda exchanging civilities and I had the impression I wasn't going to be let inside unless I passed some sort of test. Eventually he asked me into his cold kitchen. Its neat, plain style reminded me of Joyce's place. I sat down at the table but he remained standing and stayed that way for the next two and a half hours, pacing a bit and going into another room, only sitting down for the last five minutes. I didn't lose my sense of having to pass a test, which seemed at first to do with the purity of my intentions, but I soon saw it was to do with my methods. Did I have a clue what I was talking about or was I some city fool spouting stuff from books about which I had no first-hand knowledge? I realised he could see I was some sort of fool, but perhaps not irretrievable. And being local did give me some points.

I began with my research. I'd read the superintendent of the penal settlement had offered settlers a bounty for killing Aborigines, and troopers had been stationed in the district 'to quell disturbances', so, I wondered, were there any massacres around here?

'A lot of what those historians say is off the top of their

head.' Lee was immediately on fire. 'You have to go back to the journals and letters of the time. That bounty was just rumour put about by unscrupulous whites to scare the Aborigines into letting them have their land. And the troopers were here because it was the western frontier up until the 1850s. No-one knew what was beyond. There were no massacres in Wellington. I go out to the places things happened, get a feel for it,' he added, making his real point. 'People say, oh yeah, I know everything, I've read this book, but how many have been there? I have. Anything to do with Wellington, I've been there and walked around. Not just read it in a book.'

I felt put in my place. I could only acknowledge my inadequacy. What I really wanted to know was what happened in the years after early settlement. I had done some more research – from books, I hardly dared mention – about the 1850s gold rush at Wellington but not found any connection with the Wiradjuri. Were they involved in the gold rush?

'The gold rush changed things for the Wiradjuri. You've only got to think about it. Young fellas, twenty years old, born when the place was already settled. They pretty quick worked out that the whitefellas would give them money for this stuff. You have to think about what it was like then. No-one had much money, you had to be reasonably well off to even own a horse, and suddenly there was this chance of money.' Lee kept pacing as he talked, firing his words intently.

I had an image of a tall young Wiradjuri man, panning for gold, filling a dilly-bag with nuggets, taking it to the gold-buyer's tent to sell or exchange it for food. I've always thought finding gold, a lump of shiny stone from the earth, was the purest and most ancient way to make a living. It was the earth yielding up its pretty things and you just had to keep an eye out, pick the stones up or wash them out of the dirt and they were yours, treasure for the taking.

'Did they find much?'

'Same as anyone.' Lee shrugged. 'White or black, some did, some didn't.'

Then there were the Chinese, up to 5000 in the district, some of whom stayed and had market gardens along the river. The Yick Lees, the Loosicks. And later, after the goldrush, the Ah Sees and Coons. Aborigines worked for them in the gardens, which was how the Chinese–Aboriginal connection began. They were both second-class citizens, the bottom of the order, so it was natural that they would meet and intermarry. Wiradjuri did seasonal work in the market gardens through the nineteenth and twentieth centuries, the back-breaking work of harvesting vegetables. I did it one year, picking beans at Coon's market garden, but I only lasted until lunchtime. You were paid by what you picked and I was too slow.

The Aborigines were considered better workers, Lee said, especially after so many of the whites disappeared to the goldfields at Hill End. He pointed out that most of the properties were huge as squatters had seized land early on, so they needed, for instance, at least thirty men to harvest the wheat. I chipped in, feeling pleased I had something first-hand to offer, that my grandmother used to have to cook for thirty extra men at shearing time – that was as late as the 1940s.

Lee said rural work was still available for both whites and Aborigines until after the Second World War when the ready availability of trucks, tractors, hay-balers, harvesters and electrical shearing stands meant one or two men could do the work of dozens. By the time I was born, all the farms were practically family operations, except at shearing time. There was very little extra farmhand work for whites or blacks.

I mentioned farmers finding Aboriginal axes and grinding stones and spearheads in their paddocks. We had our two stone axes that Dad had found, but Tim had told me he knew of farmers with piles of them in their sheds.

'That's one of the problems.' Lee was suddenly angry. 'There's no Keeping Place around here. Nowhere safe. Not just farmers taking it. A whole lot of stuff was given to the Land Council a few years back and now it's all gone.'

'What happened to it?'

'You tell me.'

'It just needs some politician to take it up,' I said encouragingly. 'A country museum of Aboriginal culture. I saw a great one up at Kakadu . . .'

Lee cut me short. 'We've talked to everyone. No-one's interested. Big business is all that counts to them. Look at Aboriginal artefacts being under the National Parks Act instead of the State Heritage Act. The National Parks Act says you must "knowingly" disturb an Aboriginal site. Doesn't count as breakin' the law if it's not "knowingly". Ha! What's the bulldozer driver gonna say? The Act is useless.'

He was properly angry by now, his tone scathing, way past being interested in my encouraging noises. 'And anything collected before 1967 still belongs to whoever collected it. You might have some carved trees in your back shed and you can just say your grandfather gave them to you and grandfather is dead thirty years so who are you going to ask? It should be under the State Heritage Act where it could be properly protected but it's never going to happen. Miners, big business.'

His conversation swirled and veered like Joyce's and with his intensity and wired energy it was difficult to keep up, let alone try to steer him onto my track, but it seemed like an opportune moment to ask about the bora ground.

'There's a few,' he replied, suddenly cagey. 'Five I know of.'

'I mean the main one. The big one they used for all the initiations along the Macquarie River.'

'I know where it *was*. Nothin' there now. It's a ploughed paddock.'

He wasn't giving anything away so I dived in and added a bit more. 'My brother says it's just up the other side of Nanima. A few kilometres or so.'

'I could show you the documents that would tell you exactly where it was.'

I wasn't sure if that was an offer, or an 'I could, but I won't', so I dived in a bit more. 'I've got copies of all the drawings, all the carvings on the trees, you know, that, what was his name, Henderson, did originally in . . .'

'Henderson, 1832. I've got all that. I've got his book.'

'Yes, I'm sure you have, but you are saying you have a document that tells where it is?'

'Yeah, when you read his journal . . .'

'I've read it. He doesn't tell where it is.'

'Oh yes, he does! When you know the area like I do and he starts talking about five miles up this creek and down through there, you start knowin' where he's talkin' about.'

It was a strange conversation, me buzzing about like a

mosquito and him swatting me away. When I listened back to the tape I could hear the pleading in my next question.

'I know it's a big ask, but would you have time to show me where it is? Take me there?'

'Ah, no. You won't get out there. It's private property.' He was looking directly at me, but wasn't giving anything away.

'Yeah?'

'Yeah.'

Then there was silence.

'Ah,' I said in a semi-accepting tone.

More silence.

'So how can I get out there then?'

'There's nothin' there.'

'Yeah, I know. But I just want to stand there and feel it.'

'You'd have to ask the property owner.'

'What's his name?'

'Not goin' to give it to you, because I'm not goin' to give you the location. It's still very secret.'

Silence again. Then Lee made an offering.

'Partly it's the property owner, his attitude is 'it's my land and no-one's allowed on. Only about three or four property owners in this whole district with that attitude, and he's one of them.'

'My brother says he's pretty sure where it is but he won't tell me either. He's been up on the hill across the river and looked down on it.'

'I've been right on it. And you do get the feeling of it . . .'

'Yeah, that's what I want. I'd love to go back in time. Just to see it. The way it was, I mean. I know as a woman I wouldn't be allowed, but I'd still love to see it.'

He leaned forward and shook his head. 'Keeping quiet about where it is, it's a necessary evil. Advertise it and idiots would go in and wreck things.'

Well, it's already wrecked, I thought, but I knew what he meant. Other sites would become vulnerable and there weren't the means to protect them. There was no way he was going to allow me to tell the whole world where even one site was.

We talked for another couple of hours, or rather Lee talked, heading down his own tracks, while I occasionally made an inconsequential remark. In all his stories, historical and contemporary, there was an element of setting the record straight. For him, the official line would never be swallowed, not without corroborating evidence.

He showed me bits of pottery and bricks from the original penal commandant's residence; he told me about McGregor finding gold in Wellington in 1839 long before the official Hargraves 'discovery' at Ophir; he related how, in 1830, the Wellington Aborigines had a major battle with the Molong tribe and killed fifty of them; he told me about the man known as 'King Burrendong', who was 'six foot six and built like Arnold Schwarzenegger', the leader of his people, who made the Wellington Wiradjuri feared by all the other Aborigines.

Here it was again, this story of fierceness conflicting with the reports of how peaceful and relaxed they were. Lee explained that it was exactly because they had a warlike reputation that they could afford to be relaxed with the whites. 'They felt superior to other Aborigines and equal to the whites. King

Burrendong was respected by the whites, there was mutual respect.'

That sounded right. You can afford to be cool when you know you're on the top. I remembered Reverend Watson's reports of young men over six feet tall, well built, oiled black skin, naked except for the possum skin belt, and realised how physically impressive they must have been to short, sun-reddened Englishmen.

Not that their physiques did the Wiradjuri a lot of good in the long run. By the time I was born, they were not counted as citizens, needed passes to move from district to district, were not able to sit down in a pub and have a glass of beer – and they had become paler and shorter as well.

Lee believed things weren't as bad as all that. Not compared to other places. He acknowledged there was, and still is, racism – he only had to go into a shop downtown with his Aboriginal friends to see that – but generally, it was more peaceful than other places. And these days in Wellington Aborigines were employed in lots of areas – the ambulance service, hospital, local council, supermarkets. I mentioned that when I had my first weekend job at Coles in the late sixties I worked with a couple of Aboriginal sisters, the Darneys.

'Yep,' he said, 'there's no race or gender when it comes to getting jobs – it's who you know and there just isn't enough jobs to go around. Unemployment is the main reason that younger and younger kids are turning to alcohol and heroin and even ice.'

I remembered Bill Riley saying fifteen years ago that heroin had caused crime waves in Wellington. It had made me feel sick. In my twenties I had close friends who had become junkies: beautiful, clear-eyed Barbara ending up in jail; Bruce, handsome and well built, a kind of King Burrendong of our hippy gang, pasty and wrecked. Aboriginal teenagers, country kids at the beginning of their lives, being drawn into heroin because there was nothing else to do, no choices available to be made, seemed too horrible to consider. It had happened, beginning around the late seventies and, according to Lee, was still going on, with the even more insidious ice now added to the mix.

At this point Lee launched into another angry critique of how and why the government was not doing what needed to be done. 'People say we should just rid Wellington of dealers, we all know who they are, but in ten minutes there'd be another set of 'em. The government is never going to tackle the overall problem 'cos the economy needs crime. You think about it, for each criminal, maybe someone who has broken into a house and stolen a few things to support their habit, about sixty or so people are kept in work. You think about it – the glazier to fix the window, the carpenter or locksmith to fix the door, the shopkeepers to sell a new telly and computer, the cops and court people, solictors, builders of jails, warders. There's a lot of jobs that would go out the window. Crime is the fourth largest provider of jobs in Australia after mining, tourism and . . . let me see . . . agriculture. That's why nothin' is ever goin' to happen. The economy would collapse. It was a state government minister who told me that.'

He added that last comment because he must have been able to see my 'he's off on a conspiracy theory' look. It actually made sense to me, sounded true enough, but it wasn't really what I wanted. Then, before I could say anything, he branched out into what he saw as the other main problem for the Wiradjuri. It took me a while to see, but I finally realised that what he was saying, while it sounded less horrifying, was more fundamental than the drug issue. It underlay drugs and the Native Title conflict and every other problem in the Aboriginal community.

23

Elders Usurped

'The kids don't respect the elders any more,' Lee said.

It sounded like the clichéd complaint: there's no respect for the old folk these days. But before I could say anything he had launched passionately into his argument.

'The reason Wiradjuri identity held together for the last 200 years was the elders. The young kids, the teenagers, they all respected the elders. Auntie and Uncle, that's what they were called. All older people.' He went on to explain Auntie and Uncle were titles of acknowledgment and respect. Guidance, correction, judgment, decision-making – these were the rights and duties of elders.

'And it's broken down. Or breaking down anyway. That's the single thing that's wrecking everything. The elders were the government.'

It was the way all Aboriginal societies worked: respect for elders, obedience to their law. When and why had it changed in Wellington? If it had endured through the convict

settlement violence and the missionaries' attempts at indoc-
trination and the farmers' appropriation of land, what had
happened to finally break it down?

'The Land Rights Act,' said Lee flatly. 'That was the beginning of it.'

He referred to the clause that Gaynor had mentioned that
gave the right to sit on a local Land Council to any Aborigine
with residency. It gave everyone – Wiradjuri or non-Wiradjuri,
local or blow-in, young or old – equal influence. It didn't
matter whether you were a local traditional elder or a young
cluey city Koori with a paid job in an Aboriginal organisation, you still had the right to be on the council. It sounded
good – equality and democracy – but democracy in practice
is a numbers game requiring organisation and bargaining.

'None of the elders knew about that sort of thing. Numbers, deals, huh!' he scoffed. 'They simply had their authority;
they did not have to organise or make a deal with anyone to
turn up at a meeting and vote their way. The young people,
they knew how to do all that. Some of them weren't even
from the town or had been gone a long time, and gained control of the Land Council. And other Aboriginal organisations,
even Joyce's Health Centre.'

'So you reckon it was the Land Councils that destroyed the
elders' authority?'

'Land Councils – and the holy dollar,' said Lee.

There were paid jobs and corporations to organise things
that the elders had done for nothing. Fairly soon, the elders
didn't have the authority over decisions they'd had before.

'I reckon,' he said, 'the Land Councils were set up to chop
the elders out of the way. Best way to get rid of something is

to chop off its head and the elders were the head of Aboriginal society. Now it works the same way as white society – whoever can get to be the king of the castle.'

'Personal power?'

'Exactly. Same as everywhere. King of the castle.'

It was a game we played as kids, pushing and shoving to get to the top, chanting, 'I'm the king of the castle and you're the dirty rascal.' There was the pleasure of getting to the top for a few seconds and the helplessness of being pushed down and kept at the bottom. I realise now it's the children's game that most clearly and simply teaches the workings of our society. I wonder what that game would be for Aboriginal kids?

In Aboriginal society elders had shared power. They had talked over issues together and continued talking until agreement was reached rather than one person imposing a decision on the others. As Henderson had said, the Wiradjuri men argued the case for war or peace 'not as a rabble, but with the air of great speakers'. That was nearly 200 years ago in the Wellington Valley. Those speakers are gone and their descendants are not listened to anymore.

It's not that elders are finished with, certainly not in more traditional communities, but according to Lee and Joyce Williams and Jim Stanley, it's on the way out. Part of me pragmatically believes it had to happen, that the younger Aboriginals could see which way the wind was blowing. Lee agreed. He made clear that he didn't think the younger ones were bad or had any ill intent. The elders were too old to do the work now and why not have younger people who were educated in the white system paid to run things for their community. It made sense.

'But,' he said, 'the elders should have been kept on committees and corporations out of respect. And there ought to be an Elders Corporation, above all the other corporations, and all the important decisions should be referred to them. It's never going to happen now. Too many people after money and glory.'

I suddenly felt the enormity of the loss. Joyce had tried to make it clear to me, saying Rose didn't recognise her as an elder; and Jim Stanley had voiced it: *For a young girl to come along and do this to the old people.* But I realised at last that it was a great deal more than a loss of personal power and influence, it was the loss of a way of governing that had lasted for tens of thousands of years. It's not to say the elders were always wise or good – although I'm certain their communal society would have resulted in less self-interest than the Western world's individualistic one – but it did keep the show on the road for a long time. Not a person but a whole system has been usurped.

24

The Niece of Jimmy Governor

Lee's intense energy had left me buzzing. I went back to the retirement unit where my mother was waiting. She asked lots of eager questions, fascinated with what had been going on under her nose. Everyone might know everyone in a country town, but no-one knows all the stories, especially when there are two communities, each with their own tales.

I rang Rose but there was no answer. I put the phone down, relieved. It had become more of a ritual I had to practise than anything else. Then Mum and I drove to the Lion of Waterloo, the oldest pub in Wellington, built in 1842 and now the only place to get a decent meal at night. In the nineteenth century it was the Cobb and Co stop, in what was the village of Montefiores, so our ancestors would have stepped off the coach here and certainly gone in for a drink. Apart from the courthouse, it was the largest building in Wellington at the time and the most popular. It was made of vertical wooden slabs like my childhood bedroom, the adze marks still visible, had a high wooden ceiling hung with a few historical artefacts and, along one wall, a huge fireplace. A plaque proudly stated that the last duel to be fought in Australia happened outside the front door in 1854. For reasons lost in time, pistols were drawn and fired but no-one was killed. It was peaceful now; the owners were lovingly restoring the rooms one by one and their customers were quietly sipping wine and beer by the fire.

As we stood and talked in front of the crackling flames, I experienced a strong sense of reassurance. It felt tangible, like a cloak or shawl wrapped around my shoulders. William Yarnold, Ann Smith, Peter Müller, Patrick Reidy – convicts, gold-seeker and rebel – they must have all stood here by this fireplace, perhaps even at the same time. Somewhere out in the dark might have been Laureena's Wiradjuri parents, keeping warm by their own fires. None of them could have had any knowledge of my future being, but I am inextricably made of them.

Later on, back in the aluminium cabin, I stood on the veranda and stared down at the invisible river, glad of its presence. It's not that water has figured much in my life – I grew up during a long drought without ocean, lake, streams and without even running water in the house – but I was reassured to know the river was there in the dark. It had flowed through this landscape for millennia. I listened to the swirl of the current and the plop of fish and the occasional truck roaring over the nearby bridge.

There was rain in the night but by the time I awoke the sky was already crisply blue so everything felt freshly washed and flapping dry. The river was flowing strongly from the rain, muddy and swirling with sticks. From the veranda I saw something making circular patterns in the water and then a large fish leapt and fell back. A kingfisher watched from a branch above it, judging it too big to do anything about. It waited for a while then soared elegantly up the river, a flash of blue feathers shining in the light.

It would have been easy to sit there all morning but I had arranged to visit the local History Museum and later to talk to Joyce and her friend Evelyn. I gathered up my notebooks and drove into town. From the outside, the museum was familiar; it had been the Catholic presbytery when I was a child, and before my memory, the Bank of NSW. Dorothy, my mother's lively sister, the one who chased the mugger down the street, was married in the front room when it was a presbytery because she, a wilful blonde, was marrying a Protestant and wasn't allowed to marry in the church.

Inside I paid my entry fee and even in the first room felt my heart sink. The room where Dorothy had married was now crowded with mementoes of other lives. The glass cases, tables, the documents and clippings – everything looked dusty and worn out. In the room upstairs dedicated to Fong Lee's shop, boxes of Star starch and Rexona liniment and press-studs and saucepans, ordinary things that I hoped might move me, looked dispirited, as if they suspected they might all be worth nothing. Even though they were protected under glass, silk wedding dresses were thinning, gloves were wearing through, chamber pots were cracking.

There was a helpful volunteer who unlocked the little country schoolroom that had been transported whole to the grounds of the museum. It was meant to be set up as it might have been 100 years ago, but I recognised the desks with marble inkwells, the leather school bags, even the alphabet charts on the wall. Somehow, much too soon, my childhood had ended up in a museum.

I returned to the main building. In the back corridor were a few shelves with Aboriginal artefacts. It was a meagre collection: one carved tree trunk, a few spearheads and axe-heads, some grinding stones. One of the grinding stones caught my eye. It was a beautiful shape, perfectly spherical on the bottom but less curved on the top with a faint rim where the two sides met. It was a lovely thing and I went to touch it but pulled myself back.

'Oh, you can touch it. Pick it up if you like,' the volunteer encouraged.

I picked it up carefully. It was just the right weight and its curves were utterly exact under the palms of my hands as well as to my eye. I wondered how we know when a form is exactly as it must be. To be able to instantly take in the finest degree of angle and line and find it pleasing makes me wonder what we are designed for. I wondered if Kabbarrin made it. No, he would not have had the patience. Maybe it was Bungarri, the man who made the clay doll so beautifully, or perhaps one of the women.

I put it back and looked at the carved tree. I had known it was there, had found it when I interviewed Bill Riley all those years ago.

'I think that tree may be from a bora ground. Do you know of a bora ground around here?' I asked.

'I've heard something. It doesn't exist anymore.'

'No, I guess it doesn't. But I reckon there needs to be an

Aboriginal Museum to keep safe what's left. Not stuck out the back here.'

'Oh, Aborigines are not interested in history,' he said. He was well meaning, not racist. He had simply noticed that no Aborigines came to the museum and drawn his own conclusion.

It was probably just as well they didn't come. At least they avoided the hurt and shame of seeing their history stuck in the back passageway. There was no-one to blame for it; the museum volunteer was giving his time to protect local history and for him, as for most Australians, the Aborigines were a necessary and troubling part of the story of the past. He didn't notice that the museum contained only one side of the story: the artefacts of the invaders' victory and Aboriginal defeat.

I think of the objects I keep – curiously shaped stones from places I have visited, my photograph of Baron Rock, photographs of those I love, books I've read, childhood paintings done by my sons, a ruby glass jug handed down from one of my Reidy ancestors, a cartoon sketch of me in Paris drawn by a friend. These are part of the museum of myself, the things I would try to take with me if a fire swept through the apartment, the evidence of my story about who I am. They help form the distinct edges of myself. I wonder at the Wiradjuri appearing not to need to keep evidence, at least not before the Europeans arrived. They had functional objects – coolamons and string bags, and sacred objects – churinga and carved trees, but not individual collections of things arranged on mantelpieces or kept in drawers. I wonder then if their identity was less individual, more merged with each other and with place. I wonder if even their sense of self was more amorphous, more fluid, floating into casuarinas and wallabies and rocks. Kangaroo-man, magpie-woman, snake-man. Perhaps the childhood nightmare of my self disappearing into the universe would not have frightened them at all.

Because Evelyn was a resident there, I had arranged to meet with Joyce at Bellhaven, the nursing home up on the hill where my father had died. I hadn't been back there since. My mother returned once to pick up Dad's clothes and afterwards she said, 'It's so strange, I thought it was a lovely place when Don was there. Without him there, it's horrible. Just all these corridors and sick old people.' He was always the glow that lit her world, made it a rosy colour instead of her natural ironical silvery-grey shading.

I drove up the hill past my grandmother's old house, the grandmother who didn't want to be related to Aborigines. She had lived in town the whole time I knew her. Once, when someone asked her if she missed the farm, she had said, 'What? Miss cooking and cleaning up after thirty men.'

Gran Miller had no patience for nostalgia, but still, she would have hated to see the desolate mess that had once been her pretty garden. The roses, sweetpeas, stocks, pansies, poppies, alyssum, snow-on-the-mountain, all gone. The house, too, looked derelict although it appeared from the car in the driveway and a few toys in the yard, that a family lived there.

Bellhaven was past Gran's house, just below the old District Hospital sprawling elegantly across the hilltop. The District was the location of many of my mother's stories: where she started her nurse's training; where she and her friend Cayley carried a dead body out through the window so as not to disturb the live patients; where my father, diamond ring in hand – the ring that was stolen when my mother's house was broken into fifty years later – proposed 'under the pan-room window'. These days, the District is a hotel and restaurant and we occasionally have lunch in the 'veranda ward'. My mother is amused that the old mortuary is now Reception.

I turned into the Bellhaven grounds and saw that the nursing home had changed, nearly doubled in size. I didn't recognise anything in the side wing I went into, but from the first room I passed I heard Joyce's voice. She called me in and introduced me to her husband, Ned. I apologised for taking Joyce's time and he smiled and said, 'She'll be back.'

We walked along the new labyrinth of corridors to Evelyn's room. Evelyn looked up from her wheelchair, her large kind eyes taking me in with interest, but without the same alertness as Joyce. A young nurse, who had just finished helping her wash and dress, said we could take Evelyn around to one of the small sitting rooms if we liked. We could have it to ourselves.

We settled down there, me with my recorder and notes, Evelyn in her wheelchair and Joyce perched opposite. To look at, the two old friends were a study in contrasts: Evelyn plump and soft-bodied, wearing loose pants and a big blue cardigan; Joyce compact and small, smart as ever in a crisp 'mountain gear' style of jacket.

I quickly explained what I wanted: just some of Evelyn's stories so I had a better idea of what life was like for the Wiradjuri in Wellington over the last eighty years or so. To give me some idea of their side of the story.

Evelyn told me she was born at Brewarrina on the Barwon River in the far north-west of the state. 'Nearly born in a row boat on the Barwon,' she said. 'My mother was just about to give birth in the boat, but they got to the other side.'

'Who was your mother?'

'She was a Wighton and my dad was a Governor. After Bre we lived everywhere, Bulgandramine, Peak Hill, Nanima, Dubbo. And I'm back at Nanima now.'

Her family moved to the Bulgandramine Mission near Peak Hill when she was three months old. She had an early childhood memory of sitting in a carved tree waiting for her father to come home. He had to get permission from the manager of the Mission to go into town or do anything and then in 1940 the Mission closed and they all had to move into Peak Hill. It was a very prejudiced place in those days; the adults couldn't go into any of the pubs or clubs and if you went to hospital, you were put on the veranda.

'Same in Wellington,' said Joyce. 'We were always on the veranda.'

I had heard about that before, but I also remembered visiting Dad in hospital once and he was in a veranda ward. I would have to ask my mother about that.

'What about going to the swimming pool? Or the pictures?' I asked.

'We had to sit down the front at the picture hall. One time, I sneaked down the back and the manager, 'e came and grabbed me by the ear and said, C'mon, get back down 'ere you little nigger.' Evelyn chuckled. 'He called me nigger. Didn't know why he was callin' me that – I had red hair!'

'Same thing in Wellington,' Joyce chipped in. 'All the Koori kids down the front.'

'Why?' I said, embarrassed by the sudden childhood memory of being scared of the kids downstairs at the front of the pictures. We went to the pictures no more than once a year, and we had to sit upstairs. I don't remember thinking of the kids downstairs as Aboriginal, just as rough and noisy.

'Just the rules in them days,' said Joyce.

There wasn't a trace of bitterness in her voice. Both of them, so cheerful.

'It was segregation, like South Africa. Didn't you feel angry?'

There was silence for a moment, then Evelyn said, 'Not really angry. More like, it was sort of hurt. I felt *that* hurting inside, you know.'

Her eyes were pained and she said it as if I would know, but I didn't. I knew what it was to be poor and have newspaper instead of toilet paper and lino floors and to be dressed in hand-me-downs, but I didn't know our house and our clothes were shabbier than most people's until I was a teenager. Poverty wasn't seen as a problem in my family, it wasn't even mentioned except as a certain disdain for anyone who was 'flash'. But as part of a farming family, however poor, I had something the Aborigines didn't – a sense that I belonged in the main story.

'And my Uncle Andy, Andy Towney he was, he came back from the Vietnam War and he went to have a beer and he wasn't allowed in the RSL club. In Peak Hill.'

'That would have been in the 1970s! That late!'

I would have been a teenager by then, with two of my own brothers conscripted into the army. I had just become aware of the war as an issue and had attended my first moratorium march, proudly wearing my badge back at school. It didn't seem possible that kind of racism had been happening just a few kilometres away at the same time.

It didn't seem unusual to Evelyn. She continued on with her history. Her family moved to the 'Four Mile' near Molong and when she was seven or eight she started going to a white school. She remembered that there was an old teacher who loved classical music and on the first day she played Johann Strauss on one of 'those old phonograms, you know' and Evelyn loved it. Her eyes shone with remembered delight. 'I loved Johann Strauss all my life. You know that film, *Strictly Ballroom*? At the beginning? Dah 'dah dah da-dum, da-dum, da-dum. I knew it straightaway.'

I laughed and hummed the waltz beat with her. I had only recently learned to waltz myself and I told Evelyn I waltzed around the room by myself, practising the steps. I didn't tell her I had been in an apartment in Paris – that would definitely be flash.

'Didja?' She smiled.

I thought of my mother waltzing around the kitchen on the farm and seven-year-old Evelyn first hearing the Viennese melody in Molong, and me practising and counting, one two three, one two three, in an apartment on the other side of the world. There were connecting threads everywhere as much as there were gaps and disjunctions.

'But were any of the teachers prejudiced? Did they treat you badly?'

'Some of them were.' Evelyn didn't elaborate.

'We always had to go and do work outside. Gardening. Picking up rubbish. We spent most of our time outside,' Joyce chipped in.

'Yeah, we spent most of our time outside too,' said Evelyn.

To both of them, it was perfectly normal, hardly cause for comment.

'Did you like doing anything in school?'

'I liked drawing. I still like drawing. I sometimes draw the carved tree I used to wait for my dad in. I still remember it.'

'And the other kids? How did they treat you?'

'I didn't mix with other kids. My dad kept us to ourselves. He kept an eye on us. He walked me to school every day. It was a long way.'

'He was very protective?' I said.

'Yeah, he kept us in a little world of his own, you know. He wouldn't let us out. I wasn't even allowed to play with other kids except from my mother's family.'

'Why was that?

'I don't know. Maybe it was because of Jimmy Governor . . .'

'Were you related to Jimmy Governor?'

'Yeah, he was my uncle.' There was a certain tiredness and regret to her voice, as if she'd had to say it too many times.

'Your father's brother?'

'Yeah.'

Afterwards, when I listened to our taped conversation, I

could hear the eagerness in my voice. Jimmy Governor was infamous; books had been written and films had been made about him. He was a young Aboriginal outlaw who, with his brother and friend, had rampaged across the state, killing nine people by the end of it. My mother said her great aunts had told her they locked their doors and windows in fear of Jimmy Governor when it was rumoured he was in the district. He started off on a farm near Gilgandra where my father's family also had a property, killing a group of five women and children, the family of the man he worked for. The women had apparently taunted Jimmy's white wife for marrying a black man.

'Maybe if he had married from his own people it probably would never ever have happened,' Evelyn said.

Again that sense of regret and I suddenly realised she felt deep sorrow for the terrible turn his life had taken. It was all an exciting story to me, a larger-than-life thriller about someone else a long time ago, aglow with the violent romance of the past. To her it was her lovely young uncle, her father's beloved brother, who had ruined so many lives and his own. He was only twenty-five, the same age as my youngest son, and he had violently killed women and children.

'I only know what my mum and dad told me. Jimmy's wife used to go up there to the home and do some washin' and ironin' for them [the family] and old Mister, whats'isname, Mister Mawby, used to follow her home on horseback and show himself to her. And he followed her around the house saying, why had she married a black bastard. And she'd go home and tell Jimmy what happened.'

'He was pushed too far?'

'Yeah, yeah. He was starved too, wasn't given any bread for the fencin' he'd done.'

Evelyn's voice was low and sympathetic. She understood, she knew the hurting inside herself, the pain of not being regarded as fully human. Her soft face looked distressed. She had one of those natures that knows and feels the pain of others and I felt shame at my sudden leap of excitement in finding her kinship to notoriety. I had no business with Jimmy Governor. I tried to shift back.

'So, your dad wanted to protect you from what people thought of him.'

'Yeah, yeah.'

'Did it make you shy, being kept away?'

'I wasn't shy.' She drew this last syllable out to suggest she had another word. 'I really had a hate towards white people.' She said it without the least feeling of giving offence. 'It was my husband who brought me out of it. He worked for Ansett.'

Her husband, Fred, had been a local Aboriginal star, the main attraction in an Ansett Airlines tourism program in Dubbo. Tourists were flown up from Sydney and given a taste of outback Australia, including Fred and his boomerang making and throwing. He was evidently a showman by nature, outgoing, warm, funny, and people loved him.

'He used to try and get me to go to their parties and I used to say, you wouldn't catch me over there, they're your white friends, you go.' She laughed at her own cheek. 'Ahh, I wouldn't go.'

'But he talked you round?'

'Yeah, he brought me out of that shell, you know. When I

started getting involved with white people, I found they were really nice.'

'Same mix as other people anyway.'

'Yeah, yeah. It took a while, gettin' adjusted to white people.'

I shifted forward, trying to pretend that she wasn't talking about me. For a moment I had a glimpse of what I looked like from the other side.

Evelyn started recounting her earlier life. Her father worked as a farmhand and a shearers' help and was paid in rations; her mother did some housework at various places, but she couldn't remember if she was paid money or not. Her dad was Pentecostal and her mum was Catholic and she followed her mum's side because they let you dance and have a drink. We grinned together at that; the Catholics could have a drink and a dance, not like that other killjoy lot sitting with a disapproving set to their mouths.

Then she started to talk about food. By now I wasn't asking many questions, Evelyn just talked as if she had been waiting for someone to come and listen. She said she was taught to take only what she needed from the land, that if there were six eggs in the nest, you took only three; that's what white people didn't do, they just took everything. And that the thunder woke the land up in the spring and every twenty or so years there was an extra loud thunder that woke everything up. She heard one extra loud this year, she reckoned, and asked Joyce if she'd heard it, but Joyce wouldn't commit. They both joined in the discussion about cooking and eating goanna – it's cooked on the coals and it sings when it's ready. They waited for my astonishment.

'Sings?' I repeated, duly astonished.

They chuckled together. 'Yeah, it sings, sort of whistles really, when it's ready.'

They loved to eat it, and to sit around the fire and talk. They still did that sometimes. Joyce had just last week been out on a camp with the Wiradjuri women elders at The Springs on the Little River and they sat around the camp fire for a couple of days. I told them my father used to take us to the Little River to go fishing and swimming in the summer. It was only a few kilometres away, but it was exciting, somewhere different from the endless days on the farm. The thought flickered through my head that perhaps my father did have a connection to Wiradjuri places, barely remembered tales from Rosina, his grandmother. Perhaps there were ghosts of stories in his mind.

I asked Evelyn about her married life. She had met Fred at a Railway Institute dance in Walcha and married him when she was sixteen. Before that, during the war, she and Joyce had worked in Sydney for a while at a factory.

'Remember the chocolate factory,' said Joyce, laughing wickedly.

They both recalled going to dances and being shy of African–American servicemen who were in Sydney on leave. No-one had ever seen black people like them before. So confident.

She and Fred moved about living at various reserves, but she said in most places Aborigines couldn't go anywhere without permission from the manager. Not at Nanima though; Nanima was always free and easy, which was why so many

Aborigines came there. They came into town and collected their ration tickets for tea, sugar, flour and meat from the police station and then went to Knuckey's shop and exchanged their tickets. Sometimes, when Fred was away, or any of the husbands, the police wouldn't give them their tickets. They always went to Knuckey's because they would let them collect their rations without their tickets. The nuns too, at the convent, would always give them a leg of lamb, and vegetables and milk; Sister Domenica, she was good.

Most of the Wellington Aborigines, including Joyce and Evelyn at one time or another, had worked in the Chinese market gardens along the river, for the Ah Sees and Loosicks and Yooks.

'Remember the Yook girls at the show,' said Joyce, and they both laughed. Joyce explained she and Evelyn would come in from Nanima and buy new clothes for the show with their husbands' shearing cheques. They always said to each other, 'This year we will beat the Yook girls.'

'The Yook girls were the most beautiful?'

'Oh yes, they always dressed up. Looked beautiful. Let's beat the Yook girls this year, we would say.'

Joyce and Evelyn both chuckled, the full, round chuckles born of pleasurable memory.

I had a sense of having lived in a parallel universe. Although we also dressed up for the show – oh, I had forgotten about that, I always had a new dress for the Agricultural Show – I had no idea the Yook girls were the ones to live up to in Wellington. They were before 'my time', but my mother, who would have been young in the same period, had never mentioned the Yook girls either.

I also had no idea that Aborigines were getting ration tickets from Wellington police station within my own lifetime. Like the returned Aboriginal soldiers not being allowed into the RSL, it sounded like something that had happened in another century, or at least some time in the shadowy past. I suddenly realised I had retained some childish sense that whatever evil had happened in the world, it had happened well before I was born. I suppose it was a way of absolving myself from responsibility, that it wasn't something I had known anything about.

I do remember a sense that Knuckey's was not a 'nice' shop to go to and have to reluctantly admit that it might have been because of the Aborigines hanging about outside.

'Was Nanima better or worse in those days?' I wanted to try to pull Evelyn's stories together. She had circled around, like Joyce, giving me fragments rather than continuous chronological narrative.

'It was better. Houses might be better now, but it's untidy. Papers blowing about. Kids drinking. I feel ashamed.' She looked pained again and wouldn't say any more.

She talked instead about Aboriginal heroes. She thought the world of the Olympic gold medallist Cathy Freeman and Senator Aidan Young and the boxer, Anthony Mundine. Evelyn mentioned her granddaughter too, film-maker Sethie Willie, and Joyce's cousin, Michael Riley, a photographer whose work I had seen in the Art Gallery of NSW and in the Musée du Quai Branly. His photographs were of large skies and land and birds and crucifixes, spare condensed images that looked and felt like my own childhood mixture of country and ritualistic religion. I had been surprised, standing there in Paris, that his experience of growing up in the central west had been so like mine.

When Joyce criticised Mundine for having a 'big mouth', Evelyn defended him. 'It's hard for Aboriginal people to get anywhere. I admire him for getting there. It's good for us.'

She wouldn't have a word said against any Aborigines and at one point stated that there was no white culture except beer and football and Holdens. I felt defensive and thought of reminding her about Johann Strauss but realised just in time she was simply trying to say there were a few things to criticise in white culture. I kept my mouth shut.

It was late afternoon by now. We had talked for over three and a half hours and it was getting dark. I took Evelyn back to her room in her wheelchair and she opened her bedside cabinet and showed me her drawings. She told me again about the carved trees out at Peak Hill and how she climbed them and waited for her dad to come home. She showed me how she still drew the carved patterns around the borders of the drawings she did for her grandchildren. There they were in brightly coloured ink, pinks and blues and yellows, the criss-crossing and diagonals and wavy lines of Wiradjuri carvings, a protective frame around each picture.

I returned to my mother's unit, bringing a piece of coconut tart from Kimbell's Bakery to tempt her appetite. I made us both a cup of tea while she asked me questions about Bellhaven and about my conversation with Evelyn. Evelyn and Joyce were the same age as her, living in the same small town, but she had never met them. I told her what they said about

Aborigines being put on the veranda at the District Hospital and she was suddenly disconcerted.

'You know, that's true. When I was nursing there, Aborigines were automatically put on the veranda.'

'But other people were on the veranda too,' I said, defending her. 'I remember Dad being on the veranda one time when he had that ulcer.'

'Yes, other people were, sometimes, but Aborigines were always put on the veranda. As a matter of course. You didn't think about it.' She looked troubled by the realisation. 'It's terrible what you accept when that's just the way things are.'

25

Trying to Talk to Rose

I tried to ring Rose a couple more times after I saw Evelyn and Joyce. Each time there was no reply I was slightly more relieved than the time before. I was 'making an effort' but I was aligned with the other side by now and she probably knew who I had been talking to and when. On the morning before I drove back to Sydney I rang one last time. The phone rang several times and then she answered. She sounded as surprised to hear from me as I was to hear her answer. She was a little unsure, but she still refused to see me.

'It's short notice, I understand.'

I was happy enough to have a way out, but I did reiterate that I'd like to at least meet her and have a cup of tea because she was so central to the original Native Title claim. Her tone changed then, sounded more accommodating. A cup of tea might be possible next time I came up to Wellington.

After I packed up the cabin I walked to the other side of Montefiores to stretch my legs. I circled past the Lion of

Waterloo and back down along the river. Suddenly I realised I was at the junction of the Macquarie and the Bell. Somehow, in all the years, I had not been to the place where the rivers met before, had not even known exactly where it was. Here it was, the place Oxley had stood, delighted with the sight of the pretty Bell flowing into the broader Macquarie, the meeting of rivers telling Wiradjuri and white travellers alike they had arrived in the right place. I stood there, staring at the distinct line where the smaller river disturbed the forward flow of the other. My gaze shifted to the ripples and bumps caused by logs and stones and differences in the depth of the river; long bubbling striations, smooth glassy ovals that lasted for a moment, swirled, slid, reformed. Strands of willow draped on the surface caused fine lacy patterns in the flow of brown water.

I had the sudden notion I could live by a river. It was one of those thoughts that seems to separate itself out from the general constant blur, and while I knew it was impractical, I considered it for a moment. I thought of Siddhartha sitting and staring at the river and learning what he needed to know. All is change. I must have first read Hermann Hesse's novel when I was nineteen, the year after I left home. *All is change* seemed an easy concept to accept in those days. I don't imagine the Wiradjuri would have found it very comforting as the new pale tribe poured into their land and changed everything.

All my childhood, Wellington people thought Sydney was a kind of Sodom and Gomorrah. It's a usual attitude for country people to have, perhaps even universal. Several years ago, when I stayed for a few weeks in the far south of France in an old stone house at the end of a labyrinth of country lanes, quiet, peaceful, winter-bare trees making mysterious patterns against the sky, I recognised the landscape instantly; it was everything European stories had led me to desire, but the owner of the farm talked about the evils of Paris, how noisy, frantic and polluted it was. The people in Wellington used exactly the same words about Sydney.

You will either go astray or be lost in the big city, they said. No-one will recognise you. You will walk down the crowded footpaths along murderous streets fenced in by skyscrapers and no-one will know who your grandmother is, who your cousin married, where your father grew up, what your grandfather did. People will be rude to you, you will not find anywhere to park your car without paying and you won't be able to breathe fresh air, nor see the stars in the night sky. It's all true, of course. Sydney – and Paris for that matter – is a 'den of iniquity' and the air is dirty and the brilliant theatre of the night sky is a blur.

Certainly no-one here in Kings Cross knows who my grand-mother was, who my cousin married or where my father grew up or what my grandfather did. In Wellington, Joyce knew who my grandmother was before I even met her. In Wellington, even the streets and buildings tell stories about my past. One day when I was walking with my mother across the lane next to Kimbell's Bakery she suddenly remarked, 'This is the lane Aunt Millie ran down with the policeman at her heels. She was just placing a bet at the SP bookies and there was a raid and they were after her.'

Even the lanes know my stories.

Both my father and mother would have preferred their children to stay in Wellington. All the generations before us had stayed. My father had bought his few acres from his uncle;

his brother stayed on their childhood farm; his sisters married in the town. Dad spent years trying to buy a few more acres for my brothers, but he couldn't afford it and they didn't want to be farmers anyway.

I was always going to leave the place where I grew up. I cannot remember a time when I thought I would stay; I could not even imagine wanting to stay. To be trapped there was the definition of despair, of a life utterly wasted. It seemed natural to go because Imaginary Life beckoned and it wasn't going to ever reveal itself in my home town. I would have to make my stories somewhere else.

The Wiradjuri left for the bright lights too, but it seems to be different for them. When I left, that was it, I was gone; but the Wiradjuri stay away for a few months or a few years and come back to Wellington for a few months or years, then leave again and come back again. It's as if they never really leave. They are only visiting elsewhere; in their hearts they are always living in Wellington and are simply away for a bit.

I partly understand. I don't feel as if I live in the city. Wherever I go, I am just visiting; not on holiday but not at home either. But neither is Wellington home. I still have no idea where that is. And yet it is easy for me to be at home in any space. Even in a hotel room in Dublin I hang a scarf around the bedpost and drape my trousers over a chair and I'm at home. When I lived under a railway tarpaulin for six months in New Zealand with only a mattress and boxes for furniture, it was home. But in the wide world outside my small enclosures, I am still looking. Perhaps it's not even a matter of finding a home. Perhaps there are only the stories of where I have been, with or without a compass.

26

Searching for the Bora

By the time I was ready to head west again the summer had arrived. The search for solid ground ought to have seemed peripheral to warm sun on my skin, jacarandas dreaming in the sky above, but I still couldn't leave it alone. In some ways I had only come full circle, back to knowing what I knew as a child; my self planted in the ground of Wiradjuri country. It was as if that was all there was to know, but it wasn't enough. It was a whole year since the dream instruction. If I kept going, followed the instruction to the letter, uncovered every last thread, surely it would all come together, tightly woven and convincing. The stories multiplying around me felt like a web pulling me inwards but some things were no closer. I still hadn't been to the Common, I hadn't talked to Rose and I still didn't know where the bora ground was.

I didn't know why it mattered to know the site of the bora, but it felt like more than curiosity. All I could think was that something sacred had been destroyed and I ought at least find out where it was.

With some arm-twisting and telephone calls, my brother Tim finally agreed to show me what he had discovered. After doing his own research, he had talked to Lee Thurlow a few weeks after my visit. He clearly passed more tests than I did, because Lee had confirmed its exact location. I suspected Lee had recognised Tim would also rather learn from the landscape than a book.

We still wouldn't be able to stand on the bora. The landowner was not going to allow anyone to tramp over his paddocks, but a farmer across the river had a good view from the top of a hill and he didn't mind if we looked from there. In fact, Tim had already been there once and made some sketches. He knew how to look at things. I remember the spring I turned eleven and was just beginning to suspect life wouldn't always stay the same, a family of swallows built their perfect mud nests under an overhanging bank in our creek. Tim, who had just started to draw, took his watercolours one day and painted a picture of the darting swallows and their nests. I remember knowing then that although he wore glasses, he could see far more clearly than I could.

Tim and I met in Wellington and drove out along the Burrendong Road towards the town's water storage dam. We turned off onto a track and bumped along, up and down hills, over a couple of cattle grids and through gates. It was a familiar rhythm from childhood, the regular stopping and starting to open and shut gates. Tim drove because he knew the way and

I hopped in and out, unhooking the chains. The cattle on either side of the track stared at us in that unfathomable belligerent way that unnerved me as a child and still does. I was relieved when I had safely opened and shut the final gate.

The farmer, Pete Truman, was working on a tractor by the shed and stopped, spanner in hand, to greet us. He had the ruddy, weather-beaten face of his tribe and an interested, enquiring look. He wiped his oily hands on back of his dusty trousers and shook hands with us both. We chatted for a few minutes about weather and crops, establishing that we were living in the same world. He had to get on with his work but was happy for Tim to show me where the bora ground was.

We set off again, following the farm track around the base of a high rocky hill. The hill was covered in silvery-white rye grass, almost obscuring the new green from the recent rain, and there were a few pines, she-oaks and eucalypts scattered between rocky outcrops. There was nothing I could see that set it apart from other hills, but it was different in its effect. It had an atmosphere of power, although not oppressively so; more a sense of silence and knowledge. It created reverie, the dreaming 'no-thought' that Proust said he required of art, but for me comes more often from nature.

'That must be a sacred site,' I said.

Tim grinned. 'It is. See that outcrop up there, just above the pines. Pete found a large churinga stone up there. He's found heaps of stones, but this one was carefully hidden in the rocks. Really big. It must have been very important.'

'What did he do with it?'

'I'm not sure. He's got it safely somewhere.'

I didn't respond. My first thought was the churinga should

be left where it was, but then it could easily be found by someone else, someone with less respect for it. Churinga stones
carried secret and sacred knowledge and were objects of great
power. As Lee said, the lack of a Keeping Place meant that
anyone who cared enough not to throw them away was stor-
ing sacred stones and carvings in sheds and studies around the
country.

'That's where we have to go to see the bora. Past those
rocks, right up to the top. It takes nearly two hours, walking,
both ways.'

He stopped the car.

'I can't do that,' I said tersely. 'That's a four-hour walk. I
have a meeting in Sydney this afternoon and it's a five-hour
drive from here.'

I had thought we could easily walk there and back in a few
minutes. All that arm-twisting just to be left sitting in the car
gazing at a hill. I tried to hide my irritation.

'It really takes that long?'

'Yeah. We could go a bit quicker, but it's pretty steep. It
doesn't look it from here, but it is.'

'You could have told me.'

Tim didn't say anything. There was nothing either of us
could do about it. He hadn't told me how long the walk would
take and I hadn't mentioned my meeting in Sydney. I tried to
calm down. It would have to be another time.

'Anyway, can we drive a bit further around to the river?'

He could at least get me a bit closer, having led me this far
and left me with nothing.

'The bora's around the bend and on the other side. You
won't be able to see it.'

'I know that, but just to be a bit closer.'

Sometimes I act as if hills will slide meekly down in front of me if I push hard enough. Tim recognised my tone and started the car again. We drove around the bottom of the hill, bumped across a tussocky paddock and then stopped again, this time in sight of the river. There was a wide river flat, freshly ploughed, rich dark loam gleaming with the cut of the plough discs.

'Pete has found hundreds of axes between here and the river. It must have been the main camp for thousands of years.'

'Well, it's a good spot.'

There would have been fish and six-inch mussels, ducks and swans, emus and kangaroos come down to drink and graze. And edible bulbs and native fruits and wild bees. A good place to spend a few months.

I got out and walked away from the car, still feeling disappointed. Tim was right – I couldn't see the bora ground, the landscape was not going to yield to me. It was quiet and still, no wind. The warm air enveloped me. I gazed across the river and imagined an avenue of carved trees still growing in the same warm air. The hill rose to my right quite steeply and I could see there would be a good direct view from its summit.

I stood for several minutes, trying to listen and watch, but feeling demanding and urgent. The ground was uneven under my feet, hollows and hillocks sloping down to the river, lichen-covered rocks scattered about. It was pointless trying to see anything. This land had been worked by farmers for nearly 200 years; the soil had been ploughed, farrowed, raked, scattered with superphosphate, planted, sprayed with insecticide, harvested, over and over for generations. There was nothing left.

I looked up. Crows circled high in the blue. I was probably as close as any Wiradjuri woman would have been allowed to get to the bora ground. Closer probably. Perhaps that was all that would be allowed to me. I walked back to the car where Tim waited, leaning against the door. I should just back down and recognise I had already got more than I was due.

All the same, when we arrived back at the shed where Pete was still working, I asked if I could come back in a few months and climb the hill.

'I just want to have a sit for a while,' I said.

He looked at me. 'Yep, that's all right. Sometimes when I . . .' He stopped and then, adjusting the direction of his sentence, continued, 'Sometimes I go and have a sit too.'

I nodded. He didn't have to let on why he went to have a sit.

We said thank you and goodbye and bumped away up the road, opening and closing gates and slowing down for the cows, some of them now standing belligerently on the track, swishing their tails. Tim didn't say anything much. I kept twisting back and watching the hill as we drove away.

27

Not Taking Nonsense

On 15 November 2007, my mother's birthday, the land first seized in 1867 by the original Town Common Committee – including my great-great-great-grandfather, Patrick Reidy – was handed over to Rose's committee. It was reported the next day, where I read it fresh from my dream instruction, that it was the resolution of the first and longest running post-Mabo Native Title claim. But of course it wasn't a Native Title result at all. It seems like a minor distinction; after all, Wiradjuri people were granted Wiradjuri land – and it wouldn't have mattered if Joyce and the other Traditional Families hadn't made their own Native Title claim.

Each time I rang her, Joyce said the claim was proceeding, but she wasn't clear about what exactly was happening. Whenever I wanted a precise date or name, she said to ask Wayne Carr, Violet Carr's son. She said Wayne lived in Sydney at the moment and she gave me his phone number. He was actively pushing the Traditional Families claim forward.

Without him, she said, it would only be the elders and 'we'll all be dead before long'.

It was nearly Christmas 2008 so I waited a few weeks until the New Year and then rang a few times and left messages on his voicemail.

Hey bro, leave a message.

By the time I did reach him I was a little nervous.

'Joyce gave me your number. I'm one of the Millers,' I began. 'There were eight of us. You might have known some of my brothers. Out at Suntop.'

'That's out Fingerpost way?'

'Yep. We turned off at Fingerpost.'

'Any relation to Dickie Miller?'

'He was my dad's cousin.'

'Ah, well, he was married to my sister-in-law Claudia.'

I relaxed, that wasn't too difficult. He would talk to me now. As a child I had only seen Dickie when he sometimes did the shearing at our place. As a pretentious teenager I had ignored him, then I hadn't seen him for years. I had met Claudia at the Health Centre when Joyce first claimed she and I were related, and that was it. I wouldn't have imagined that, one day, I'd be thanking Dickie Miller for giving me the right connections.

We arranged to meet during school hours. I already knew Wayne was looking after his two school-age grandchildren and I didn't want to get in the way.

Wayne was waiting for me on his veranda when I arrived, the same way Lee Thurlow had been. I liked it. It looked welcoming, as if he couldn't wait and had to stand eagerly outside his front door, although I did know it was to observe me before I entered his house – and that too seemed a sensible thing to do. You get no sense of a person beforehand if you just wait inside; you need to see him or her coming towards you.

We shook hands on the veranda and assessed each other. He looked about the same age as me, tall and lean with the easy manner of someone who is used to being attractive but doesn't play on it. I realised later that physical beauty was something that mattered to him; he mentioned it several times as we talked. He had a boyish air, a quick gaze and a kind of unguarded interest in the world. He reminded me immediately of one of my brothers, the one who is a blokey Buddhist. Like him, Wayne had a relaxed intensity and seemed utterly without my cursed desire to impress. Perhaps it was just that he wore shorts and t-shirt for every occasion as my brother did, but he felt so familiar I could hardly keep from exclaiming.

The front door of his Erskineville worker's cottage opened straight into a small lounge room dominated by a huge flat-screen television. As I walked in, alert to being alone in a house with a stranger, the image on the screen was of a meerkat in its characteristic surveying pose, neck stretched up, head swivelling. It looked so like a reflection of me, I nearly laughed. Wayne didn't offer to turn the television off, or even turn the sound down, and I worried it might be seen as bossy to ask, so for a while we talked under the sharp, faultless gaze of meerkats.

Although I hadn't seen anything about him in the newspapers, Wayne had been involved in the land claim struggle for at least twelve years. Everyone I had talked to referred to him as a source of historical knowledge, so, with a few precise questions, I thought he would fill in the gaps. I should have known by now that I was going to get a whole set of other stories instead. When I listened to the tapes of our conversation afterwards, and waded through at least a dozen pages of scribbled notes, I had a sensation of stepping not onto the straight path I was hoping for, but into a swift flowing river full of sharp bends.

At first, Wayne covered much the same territory as Joyce. It was Joyce who had alerted him to Rose's claim. He had been in Sydney for a few years and she had rung him up. It was the phone call that changed his life, he said. It was a statement that meant a lot more than I noticed at first and he circled back to it later.

'Why'd she ring you?'

'I had a reputation in Wellington for not taking nonsense from anyone, especially not from non-Traditional Families.'

As far as he knew there had not been any public meetings called about the claim. The first contact he had from anyone was when he was co-ordinator of the Wellington Lands Council and a genealogist arrived wanting to know his family tree.

'I wasn't right up on it then, but I did know my mother and grandmother were traditional women from the Valley, Stuart-Mickeys, directly descended from the oldest recorded families in the Valley.'

I nodded, noting how he said 'the Valley', not Wellington. It made me think about it differently, a geographical area that had been there forever instead of a town.

'Johnnie Stuart was the first Wiradjuri to be given a white name. The army bloke, William Stuart, said, look mate, you're not a bad sort of a bloke, I'm gunna give you my surname. It's in his diaries. And Michael Mitchell Mickey got his name from Mitchell, the surveyor. I don't know what their traditional names were.'

When he knew about the claim, he went off to meetings, at first 'naively and innocently agreeing to things' until he realised 'the wrong people were the major players'. Like Joyce, he pointed out the Ah Sees were Maori-Chinese originally, and the Bells only had rights through marriage to the Stanleys and so, by Aboriginal law, the Bells had to have the Stanleys' permission to say or do anything. I had heard all this before, but Wayne had taken his objections further. Because the Ah Sees signed a statutory declaration about their Aboriginality, at a meeting of the State Land Council he accused them of perjury before the Federal Court. It was an open invitation to the Ah Sees to sue him, but they ignored the invitation. Evidence, Wayne reckoned, that they knew they would lose.

He also took accusations against Rose further. There was one story that intrigued me because it showed a Rose completely at odds with the picture I had formed of her. It was during one of the mediation meetings at the courthouse in Wellington. Wayne wasn't sure of the judge's name, but he was 'a skinny sort of a little fella'.

'Justice French? Or was it Tim Moore, the mediator?'

'I dunno. A skinny fella anyway. I said to him, Your Honour, ask Rose Chown if she advertised the meetings letting everyone know about the Native Title claim. He said, Mrs Chown, did you advertise the meetings? She said, Yes, I did Your Honour. He said, Do you have proof, Mrs Chown? She said, Yes, I have Your Honour. He said, Can you go and get it now? And then she started to cry. Whenever things got a bit tough, she'd cry.'

'And the judge fell for it?'

'He fell for it. "Don't worry, I accept your word," he said.'

'It's odd that she cried. A big strong woman like that.'

'Nah, she's little.'

'Really? I thought she was large – and impressive.'

'Nah. She's little. She's about your size.'

I'm a little over five foot tall and my physical presence is not one anyone would remark on. I wondered how I could get it so wrong. From the way she out-manoeuvred me every time I rang her, and from her lounging presence on the video Gaynor had loaned me, I still couldn't imagine her as anything less than a large, powerful woman.

Wayne said she didn't know how to conduct herself. He used phrases like that: 'conduct herself'. He said she offended people she should have kept on side, recounting how she told some Stanley kids to clear off the Common. This was adding insult to injury since she only had rights to land via the Stanleys in the first place. Wayne reckoned she said she would call the police and have them charged with trespass.

His most inflammatory accusation was about money. It was much the same story as Joyce hinted at, but again, Wayne took it further. He was clearly unafraid of a public fight.

'I contacted funding bodies to see if the funds Rose had been given were properly acquitted and they couldn't tell me if they were.'

'Who gave her the money?'

'Department of Land and Environment, I think. Anyway, at our local Land Council meeting, I accused Rose of mishandling funds. It was deliberately defamatory. I had no proof whatsoever that she misappropriated funds. All I knew was that she was given over $250,000 altogether from various bodies to revegetate the Common. Planted about thirty trees, eaten by cows. Where did it all go?'

'I can't repeat that.'

'Yes, you can. It was on the front page of the paper. The *Wellington Times*. Wayne Carr says such and such.'

'Already in the public domain?'

'Front page. It was a perfect invitation to take me to court.'

'When was that? I'll check it.'

'Yeah, you check it. It was a few years back. They're a lot more careful with money they give away these days.'

I did check. The headline on the front page of the *Wellington Times*, 28 November 2003, says: 'Council Seeks Common Ground'.

> Wellington Shire Council has been told it risked signing the town's Common over to non-traditional owners who had not accounted for the expenditure of thousands of tax-payer dollars.
>
> Local Aboriginal activist Wayne Carr, who addressed Council on Wednesday night, asked councillors to consider whether they wanted to be seen to be endorsing something from which funds had been misappropriated . . .

It was a direct and public accusation, but the council's response seems irritated rather than outraged.

> 'This matter has been going on for eight years now and Council thought it had been dealt with,' Councillor Trounce said.
>
> 'This Council has bent over backwards to answer

queries for the State Government and has encouraged a resolution. Council was never given an opportunity to say who the correct people were . . . Council has no legal or moral ability to interfere with the State Government.'

The council went on to say, rather helplessly, that they would, however, find out who to write to and raise the two issues: 'the involvement of non-Wiradjuri Aborigines and the stigma of claims about misappropriated funds'.

I also found a letter published two weeks later from Vivienne Carr, chairperson of Rose's committee. She referred to Wayne Carr's 'unsubstantiated allegations' and said she had sought legal representation. She called the allegations 'vicious' and wondered scathingly about Mr Wayne Carr, who saw himself as both 'an accountant privy to confidential documents and a genealogist who knows all about Aboriginal descent'.

It is more than five years since these accusations and the exchange of threats. Apparently there was nothing more forthcoming from the 'legal representation' and no public rebuttal at all from Rose.

When I got back to Sydney I asked the main funding body about the acquittal of the largest grant and eventually received dozens of pages in reply. Much of the material was considered too sensitive to release, particularly to do with paying wages and the internal costs of the committee. It was impossible to tell either way if funding had been properly spent, but there were no obvious issues or questions.

At the same time I discovered another article about Rose being harassed by youths, who pulled down a fence she had put on the Common and hurled rocks at her tin hut. Despite everything Wayne had said, I couldn't help thinking Rose might not be entirely in the wrong. It wasn't fair at least, to only have one side of the story.

Wayne continued with his looping, repeating saga of struggle. He had been writing letters to the Department of Aboriginal Affairs and the Native Title Tribunal and Native Title Services and the State Land Council for years. He had been knocking on doors and going to meetings and attending court hearings lodging objections, arguing the case for more than a decade.

'I've kept at it like a dog,' he said. 'Native Title Services told me they wanted to use a successful outcome for Rose's mob as a model for Native Title outcomes. I wasn't going to let our country, our land, be the basis of a model for the dispossession of all Aboriginal people. It was a model of extinguishing connection to country and identity, cultural breakdown, forced assimilation.'

I didn't know what he meant at first. Surely Aboriginal land rights were about supporting connection to country and distinguishing the rights of Aboriginal people, not assimilation, but as he went on to talk about himself as a Wiradjuri man, I suddenly realised he meant the assimilation of the many separate Aboriginal identities into one. He talked about Wiradjuri history, about King Burrendong and how the Wellington Wiradjuri were the most feared tribe in the whole of the west. His voice had changed tone, not exactly hardened but it had become more intense, fired by emotion. This was coming near to the heart of the matter for him, the place that gave meaning to everything he did.

'We are the traditional people of the Valley. Have you seen the Common Agreement? It says Rose is a trustee, that she is holding it in trust for the Wiradjuri. She has no rights. You know Pine Hill on the Common, near the tip? We called it Devil's Hill, its traditional name was Yugagal – it's a most important sacred site. It's the home of Wandong. Here we got a person with no rights as Keeper of the Hill, which is one of the most important spiritual sites. I said to the registrar of the Land Rights Act, it's your job to uphold the integrity of the Act. I'm not gunna let you alone until justice is served here.'

'So where are you up to with it then? I know your lot has made your own Native Title Claim?'

'Yeah, the Traditional Families claim. We called ourselves the Gallagabang Corporation an' put our claim in 2007 or maybe it was the end of 2006, you can check, and this year we just got a new lawyer, Phillip Tietzel. Absolutely brilliant bloke, he used to work in Darwin. He's worked on these sort of cases before.'

'So is the claim registered?'

'It's goin' through pre-registration tests. It's been going back and forth for a while now. The Native Title tests . . .' He shook his head in exasperation. 'Askin' questions like do you stand naked in the river an' fish. We're contemporary Aborigines, they're not taking changes into account. And language. No-one speaks language in Wellington anymore. I'm learnin' it now. The last person I knew that did was my Auntie Martha Daley. She was what we call a "clever woman". People still marvel at some of the things she could do.'

'Was she related to Lester Daley?'

'Lester? She was his grandmother.'

'I went to school with him. He sat behind me in class and we talked all the time.'

'You'd know Neil Harvey too then? And the Steins?'

'One of my brothers was married to Helen Stein.'

The Steins were Aboriginal on both sides of the family, although Helen didn't like to identify as Aboriginal even though her Nana Smith was black. I remember her telling me one day to be careful of the 'Abos' down in the park and another time she told her mother, who was 'dark', not to speak to her when she served table at a ball Helen was attending.

'There was three of them Stein girls.'

'Yes, that's right. Helen was the middle one, the prettiest. My mother was friends with Pat, their mother.'

The conversation had shifted gradually and easily into a different register. He knew where I fitted in the pattern of families in Wellington, I wasn't just a random person unconnected to anyone or anything. I had been identified – and I suddenly wondered if my identity wasn't who I was, but what I was part of.

I settled back more comfortably in the chair. There was a different feeling between us, a warmth and ease. Wayne was in charge of the conversation but he listened intently. He spoke like an orator, impassioned and articulate, often with the unusual turns of phrase and mispronunciations of someone who has taught himself.

It felt odd that I had not met him before. He was almost exactly the same age as me and had grown up in the same small town; we must have passed each other in the street dozens of times.

28

A Wiradjuri Man

Wayne's mother was Violet Stuart, 'a very fine-looking woman', he said several times, and his father a Norwegian who didn't stick around. He was raised mainly by his grand-mother at Nanima and went to the Nanima school where he was taught by Jim Cahill right through primary school.

'Joyce says he was a good man,' I said.

'He had a lot of faith in me. He wasn't a bad sort of a fella. He made me stay in and study when the others were playin'.'

'I bet you didn't like that.'

'I didn't mind then. I won a scholarship for high school in town. The government paid for my uniform and everything. I was in the top six students out of eight classes [that's at least 200 students] for the first three years of high school. Then I just went walkabout. If you're smart enough, you know when you're being patronised. This identity thing caught up with me. I went crazy, berserk.'

I wanted to ask what he meant by 'identity thing' and

'berserk'. I supposed he was talking about Aboriginal identity, but it sounded like there might have been something else to it. He kept talking. I waited.

'I met my missus when I was sixteen. Together thirty-nine years.'

'Is she a Wiradjuri woman?'

'No, she's a Kempsey woman.'

'That's a long way from Wellington. How did you meet her?'

'They had these Aboriginal dances in George Street in Sydney. It was '69. Her uncle was a singer in the band and she came along to listen to him. A lovely-looking Aboriginal girl. She was sixteen when we first got together and nine months later we had a baby. I just couldn't handle it. Didn't realise I'd found my perfect partner right then and there. A very attractive woman, a highly intelligent woman, the most natural mother, a wonderful, caring nurturing woman. I just didn't wake up to it. I just didn't wake up to it. I just didn't wake up to it.'

She must have left him, I thought. Who has such regrets when their beloved is still around?

'I'd go walkabout for a year, two years. And walk back into my house, my wife, my kids – and she treated me with the same affection. She said to me, I know who you are. She understood me. I was a wild child, a wild man. Oh yeah, a madman, a complete madman.'

'What do you mean? Breaking the law?'

'Absolutely. Doin' things I should'na done. Beltin' people. Smashin' people. Everywhere. In Wellington. And Sydney.'

'Did you feel chaotic?'

'Absolutely mental. Absolutely mental.'

There was a weight to these words, to the whole turn the conversation had taken and I kept feeling I was talking to my Buddhist brother who also went through mental torment for nearly a decade. Many seasons in hell. There was the same steady weight of pain, past now, but long and hard enough to have formed an iron anchor in his soul.

There was a silence. He was making up his mind about something.

'You reflect back on why you behaved that way. See . . .'

There was another longer silence and I realised he was going to show me the wound. I felt nervous but I was used to it; it happens all the time in writing classes. I sometimes think writing is a kind of surgery of wounds, cleaning them out and, with any luck, stitching the skin delicately back together.

'You see, I feel like I can say I'm a fairly intelligent fella. I know that. And as you get older, you don't get wiser unless you reflect back and start making adjustments, to address your past. If you don't, it shows you were a dummy. So, I was thinkin' about my past life, things I blotted out of my past history.'

A silence again.

'You see, I was molested when I was seven or eight.'

There it was. A childhood pierced and drained out. The worst of it is, it's a wound that never properly heals. I didn't want to ask him who, or what happened. It wasn't my business. The details come unbidden to my mind anyway. It has happened in our family too, some of our children abused, and I know how it undoes people. It's the utter disregard for the separateness of another's being, it's as if you just don't count.

'I was all right and then when I was sixteen . . . you reach a certain age and you start reflectin' back. You remember. And you have your first drink, and you rebel.'

'It's happened in my family. I know.'

'I'm amazed I never got locked up for killin' someone.'

'Or yourself.'

'Yeah. You think about it. You try to blot it out. Use drugs. Alcohol. I had all these wonderful opportunities – lost. All these teachers ringin' my grandmother – she reared me up, very strict, very stern, urgin' me back to school. I wouldn't go back. Then, as I said, I got together with my missus and had a baby nine months later. Couldn't handle it. I treated my family pretty badly. I was there for them, when I was there, but when I was drunk, I went crazy. I set them a bad example with my missus . . .'

'When did it change?'

'When I was thirty-seven.'

I was struck by the odd precision of it. As if he woke up one morning and everything was different.

'What happened then?'

'I think it was just maturity. It took me a long time, right through from when I was sixteen until thirty-seven. It didn't change right away. I reflected about things and I started to change for the better. Then probably the most significant thing after that was the phone call from Joyce. A frail little woman, eighty-four, but a fighter. I love her, I'd die for her.'

I did some quick arithmetic and realised he must have been in his early forties then. Wayne had received a phone call that changed his life and gone back up to Wellington and got stuck into the Native Title fight around the time I was saving up to leave Australia and stride around Europe in my flapping coat.

'But my daughter, she's a drug addict. Two kids. And their father was too. Both drug addicts. Uncivilised, both of them.'

I started to ask what he meant by 'uncivilised', but he was in the full steady flow of a story that had to be told.

'I happened to be in Sydney when the father died. His family was Italian, wealthy family, and they said, well, what are we going to do with these little blackfellas? I said I'd look after them. I wouldna done it if I hadn't got involved in this Native Title business. This struggle has reinforced me, not just as a person, but my Aboriginality. It brought out my Wiradjuri spirit. Too many Aboriginal people have forgotten it's part of Aboriginal culture to look after kids in this situation. It's my responsibility to look after them, discipline them, re-educate them. They were uncivilised when I got them, no manners. They appreciate now they've got someone in their corner to protect them – I do the washin', ironin', cleanin', cookin' – I even did a cookin' course so I'd know how to do it properly.'

There was just a little pride about the cooking course, the first I had heard. For the rest, he was simply recounting what had happened, what needed to be done. I wondered again about his wife, where she was, why he was looking after the kids on his own. And his daughter, where was she?

'A better dad this time?'

It was none of my business. I shouldn't have asked. I could feel the sting of resentment at the prodigal's return. I hadn't belted anyone, smashed anyone, walked out on my kids – why was I the one who had lost the way?

'Without a doubt.' There wasn't the faintest trace of desire to defend himself. 'This is the sort of dad I should have been. These children brought out another aspect of the journey. Absolutely brilliant. These kids were uncivilised. The girl, she's an alcohol syndrome child. A wonderful, lovely little lady now. The boy, he's ADHD. No sugar, tea, coffee, sweets in this house . . . It's made me realise what I had missed out on with my kids – and what I had done to my wife, wandering out, causing all this commotion. I'd be away for a year, or two. She is just this most remarkable woman. Just this rock-solid individual female.'

His voice was intense, the broad Aboriginal accent flattening the sound and giving his praises an almost mesmerising sound. I couldn't look away from his eyes.

'She was looking after them, she's a drug and alcohol counsellor, but this wonderful woman, she couldn't handle these kids. The boy, he was a misogynist at six years old. Wouldn't treat her with respect. It was making her sick. I said, the best I can do for you, darlin', is, I'll look after the kids. I'll get another place, we'll visit and you recuperate. I know how hard it was for her now, bringing up our kids.'

'She lives nearby?'

'Yeah. I take the kids 'round there sometimes. The girl, she wants to see her mother, but her mother's in jail. If she's not in jail, she's in rehab and then she's usin' again.'

'What was your daughter's problem?' I knew the answer and wondered why I had to make him say it.

'It was me.' There was no self-pity, no asking for forgiveness, just a simple acknowledgement. He had failed as a father and he took full responsibility for the mess of her life. The clear light of his truth-telling felt like some kind of grace.

'She was absolutely beautiful, gorgeous, highly intelligent, same intelligence as her mother. Sandy blonde hair, olive skin, eyes of four colours according to the weather – light brown, to light green, to dark green, to blue. People would stop us in the street and say they had to take a photo. Now she's a lost cause.'

'Not really. She could change.'

'No. She's a lost cause. She's a lost cause.' He said it over and over, his voice flat.

I didn't want to agree with him. All those gifts, all that beauty and intelligence. That child with the four-coloured eyes who had come through him into the world, sitting blankly in a cell or on the street somewhere. There should be a chance for her. Sometimes there is too much pain and it doesn't make you stronger, it just wounds you forever.

'So it's your grandkids now.'

'Yeah. They have to be educated and know Aboriginal law. They have to go into the future with their identity intact.'

We both sat for a bit.

I wondered about second chances and whether everyone gets them or not. Whether a whole country gets another chance to do things right and whether it ever makes up for doing it so badly the first time.

'I often sit down and reflect back on my life and every aspect of it has been a fascinatin' journey, a fascinatin' life.' Wayne was gazing intently, not at me, but a focused, short-distance gaze as if he were seeing his life on a screen just in front of him. 'When you look into it, it's just been a typical Aboriginal person's life. All the hardships, all the opportunities let go. I'm so glad it's all happened to me, because it's made me who I am now.'

29

Identity

It was the middle of the afternoon, quiet and hot, the gauze door filtering the summer light. 'Shut the wire door,' my father used to yell when we ran into the house. I could hear the rattling bang and click of the door in my mind still. I felt the faint acrid pang of envy. Wayne believed his story so passionately; for me there was a gap, I was always the observer. I couldn't do without my story but I didn't merge with it the way he did.

Did that mean Wayne knew who he was and I didn't? Each of us was made of threads from different parts of the world but we had been born and grown up on the same land. I wondered what difference it would have made if his Norwegian father had taken him back to Norway and brought him up with Viking tales and fjords, snow falling at dusk and Ibsen. Or if my ancestors had stayed in Ireland and I had grown up in Limerick with green fields and stony villages and studied at Trinity. Even with the same genes, the story could so easily be different; a series of random chances that determines where the cloak of identity is hung.

There was a feeling of no-one else being in the street, of just us and our conversation. I imagined it was always that way around Wayne, that his intensity pulled everyone's attention towards him, but that his attention ranged out restlessly across streets and cities, all the way across the country to his childhood and back to the corridors and offices of power that seemed to be obstructing his people's future. His conversation circled away from his own family, his grandchildren and his care of them, back to the wider Aboriginal community, the politics of land and power, but it was clear it was a continuum to him. It was always about protecting Wiradjuri identity.

Wayne's assessment of Aborigines involved in 'the dispossession industry', as he called it, was blunt. He reckoned that Aborigines in the system were supporting a government agenda that, as he'd pointed out, was not protecting identity but encouraging assimilation. He said they were interested only in keeping their generous pay packets. I couldn't imagine Wayne was ever afraid of a fight, but I didn't really want to get into that territory. I tried to return to the thread of the Wiradjuri land claim.

'So is the Traditional Families claim over the Common?' It was a rhetorical question; no-one had suggested it was anything else.

'Nah, nah. It's big, an area 100 by 130 kilometres.'

'Really! That sounds like a large part of the central west!'

Wayne explained that it extended from near Dubbo in the north to near Molong in the south, and from the Hervey Ranges in the west to Eulan in the east. My childhood farm was part of it, although of course Native Title did not extend over freehold land. I suddenly realised that meant it did not extend over Rose's freehold land either. It seemed too confronting to point that out and ask him what he therefore thought Native Title would actually give the Traditional Families, so I said nothing. I would ask later.

'But the Common is the most important part of it. It's the only piece of untouched tribal land in the Wellington Valley. We're not going to build anything on it, do anything to it. We want to leave it.'

I wondered again what power he thought he would have to control what Rose did, but changed tack.

'What about Aboriginal artefacts though? A Keeping Place? Wouldn't you want to build a Keeping Place? I know farmers have collected a lot of things over the years.'

'We're going to negotiate to get them back and build a cultural centre.'

He started explaining his plans for the future, including the reconstruction of the convict settlement at the Maynu Gagnal site, to be used as an Aboriginal cultural centre. It seemed neatly circular to him to reclaim the site of the first invasion of the Valley as a place to tell Wiradjuri history and culture.

'That would cost a lot,' I said sceptically.

He grinned. 'I figure the land they took from us, the 100 by 130 kilometres, might be worth, say, a billion dollars. All we want is a few million back, then we could do everything we want. Study the benefits of native fruits, buy a property and grow the trees, set up a small factory to make juices. We have to start negotiating.'

It sounded solid, hopeful. I couldn't see any government

giving them a few million dollars any time soon, but there was no point in saying it. Wayne was clearly going to stay on the case as long as he had breath. His energy seemed unstoppable in the face of constant knock-backs, generated by a kind of obsessive machinery that wouldn't let him rest.

'So what keeps you going?' I didn't mean it so much as a question, but as an acknowledgement of his endurance, but he shifted forward in his chair and looked at me intently.

'Identity,' he said, 'because identity is the most important thing. It gives you self-esteem, it gives you something to live for.'

I shifted forward myself. It felt as if the words were being addressed to me, an instruction, as if he were telling me my problem and its solution; that somehow he had seen into my embarrassingly empty soul and knew what had caused it. I had lost track of my identity and I needed to find it.

Didn't I know that already? It felt strangely like I was hearing it for the first time. The amorphous inner state seemed exactly named as it never had been before. There was an authority in the tone of his voice, in his compelling gaze, giving the words a different weight and texture. I suddenly knew that sometimes, in the middle of the afternoon, you could properly hear the truth.

'With our 40,000 years in this country,' Wayne went on, 'we cannot allow a little moment in time to break that down, to bring it to a full stop.'

It was continuity of identity he was talking about, the continuity of culture in relation to place. He knew who he was because of this particular place. His ancestors had lived by this river on this land for tens of thousands of years and that knowledge coursed through him, made fire in his veins and his heart, illuminated him. For him it was the fight to regain this land that gave his life shape and meaning. I thought about my family's connection, especially my father's as he walked over the farm or sat on the kerosene tin in the backyard, his face uplifted, receiving benediction. I remembered him saying once that there was nothing like the joy of working the soil to provide food for others. For my father the meaning was nourishment, literally.

My story was about the town and the family I came from and the Wiradjuri land I was born on, and so was Wayne's, each of us reaching down into other continents, but always coming up into the light in this soil. Without it, we could not survive.

'The Wellington Valley is the most important place in the whole of Wiradjuri country.' Wayne's voice was more intense, almost ringing, as if he were addressing thousands instead of just me in his lounge room in Erskineville. 'The whole Wiradjuri nation was born in the Valley. Baiame came out of the sea in the east on his emu feet, a giant of a man, with his two wives, and he strode up through the Valley and he created it. It's the most important place. It's where the stories come from. That's why I won't let it go. I won't let it go.'

As I drove home afterwards, the sentence kept coming back to me: *it's where the stories come from*. I knew Wayne meant that all stories originated in the Valley, and even more specifically, that they were the stories of origin, of creation, itself. They were the creation stories of his people, the stories of Eden. 'I come from the place the stories come from', rang in my head like a chant. It felt like an extraordinary gift; what I had been looking for and hadn't known was there. I was born where stories were born.

That night, in the early hours before dawn, the few short hours in Kings Cross when the streets fall silent, I awoke and heard *I come from where the stories come from*. The sentence simply appeared as I woke up, as if it had been trying to force its way through layers of dreamy sludge and had to wake me so I would hear it. It was a simple reiteration, but a sentence that arrives in the middle of the night is useful, as Anthony said. The words sang through me. They felt different, vibrating with a particular force.

I lay in the stillness of the night and realised that in the dark labyrinth of the unconscious, the words had expanded and shifted and found a new meaning. I suddenly knew that underlying everything – the patterning of memory, Wayne's passionate journey, the town's history of convicts and missionaries and gold-seekers, and even under the Wiradjuri landscape soaked deep in my cells – underneath it all was storytelling itself. It was telling the story that joined me together, joined us all together. In the moonless night a core of knowing formed in me, and what I knew for certain was that identity and connection could only be found in the telling. It wasn't the threads of the story that really mattered, it was the weaving of the threads.

It was so quiet I could only hear Anthony breathing. The night wind from the harbour that often rattled and knocked at the old sash windows had died down. It didn't matter that there might be darkness on either end of life and infinite space all around when there were stories to weave. If they thinned and faded then it was time to get up and start restoring the colours and threads. I thought of my father and his ancestors all dead and gone, and my mother, old and frail in Wellington, and all my brothers and sisters scattered around the countryside, and Wayne and Joyce and Evelyn and Rose, all with their own stories. By history and chance and long ancestry I am from Wiradjuri country and I am part of its story.

30

Who Belongs?

Just before I left, Wayne and I had an argument. I had been going to pick on a few things he said, but each time reminded myself I was there to listen, not argue the point. Then he said something that undid my disciplined intentions.

'You can't take country out of me. You can't take country out of the man,' he said.

'Or woman,' I said. 'I go back to Wellington often because my mum still lives there and whenever I go back, it's like the country knows me.'

Wayne looked at me, all his attention focused. 'I know how special you feel about it, but it's more special to me.' He said it as gently as he had said anything all afternoon, but I still wasn't going to let that go.

'I don't think you can say that. I know about country. And you can't know if one person's feeling is more than another's.'

'Whitefellas say they own country. We don't say that. We say country owns us.'

'I know it's not about owning. I know that.' I felt impatient. Who did he think I was? 'We don't own anything there anymore, but it belongs to us. My dad, he had a breakdown and sold our farm and afterwards he didn't remember what he had done and he said, how could I have sold that land? I love every inch of it. I know the difference between owning and belonging. We don't own anything, but we belong.'

'Your dad loved it, but whitefellas don't have the connection that Aboriginal people have.'

'No-one can say what other people are feeling. You can't know that. And you can't know whether it's any more or less than someone else's feeling.' My dad's unproven line of Wiradjuri inheritance came into my mind.

'I believe if your culture is developed to the extent of that connection to the land Aboriginal people have, you can say it, you can make that distinction,' Wayne said firmly.

'You can't know anyone else's inner feeling. You can't say you love someone or something more than someone else.' I was repeating myself.

'I think you are wrong.'

'That's all right, you're allowed. But I still don't believe you or anyone else can know what my dad or anyone else felt.'

'There were "clever men" in Aboriginal culture with trainin' to the highest level. They knew people's inner thoughts and feelings. They would know.'

'Yes, well, maybe. I'll grant that could be possible.'

We had reached the end of it. Neither of us had convinced the other but it felt all right. We were from the same land and it didn't matter too much that we weren't going to agree about whose connection was greater. And, truthfully, it was an old argument for me, not enough anymore.

Wayne had been finding out about 'clever men' and Wiradjuri spiritual beliefs.

'I love it,' he said. 'Our Wiradjuri religion.'

He talked about the Henderson drawings of the carvings on the bora ground and there was a different air about him, no longer fiercely certain but questing, excited. He was uncovering the lost stories of his people, an explorer in his own culture. I recognised the thrill, the pleasure of knowledge in the way he talked. His eyes were eager, his voice warm, like a boy full of the delight of discovering new territory and the joy of knowing it was his own long lost place. There was treasure in his land that he hadn't known was there.

He told me about the cave paintings in the hills around Wellington and the Wiradjuri names of landmarks, each of them formed by Baiame. Mount Arthur out along Bushrangers Creek Road was called Moreebna, and nearby were Irribung and Durra. If you looked down from the top of Durra or Irribung, Wayne said, you could see a 300 metre human footprint – five toes and all – in the landscape, evidence of Baiame's journey. I remembered the strange air that Bushrangers Creek Road always had, the feeling of danger and discovery.

We had been talking for a few hours and I knew his grandchildren would be home soon. I wondered if I should leave before they arrived in case they were put out to see a stranger in their lounge room, but just as I was packing my notes and the cassette away, they walked in. They were beautiful-looking children, neatly dressed in fresh blue and white school uniforms, both with an eager story to tell as they came in the door. They were disconcerted to see me, but they acknowledged me and, under Wayne's watchful eye, greeted me politely.

He stood up to show me out. His rangy body and focused air again brought my brother to mind and I gave in to the desire to exclaim. After all, I knew something about his life now.

'You remind me so much of one of my brothers. As soon as I saw you. You have the same look, the same air. He's had a hard time and now he's found a way for himself. He's gone off into Buddhism.'

We were both back out on the veranda now, above the shimmering summer street. The city was all around us, stretching in every direction for as far as we could walk in a day. We exchanged a look, knowing we understood each other. He grinned.

'And I've gone off into the Dreamtime.'

31

Australia Day

Late summer had taken hold in the city: black bitumen streets radiating heat, limbs bare and brown, cool surf beckoning and beer on suburban verandas. It felt like time to stop searching, to slip into the green sea water, but I wanted to talk to Lee again and I needed to walk on the Common, to see finally what the fight was all about. It had become mythological and I needed to feel its ordinary soil, its grasses itching my ankles. And there was still Rose.

Rose lived on the Common and if I was ever going to talk to her, that's where I would have to go. Everyone I had spoken to was on 'the other side' and they had all spoken ill of her. In fairness, I had to hear her point of view, but over the year I had aligned myself with the opposition. I believed in the rightness of their claim and that Rose was in the wrong. If I were to ask her questions, she would have to know where I stood.

I started ringing her in the morning and on the final

attempt that evening she answered. I said I was coming up to Wellington and was hoping we might have that cup of tea and a piece of cake.

'You've rung a few times now,' she said, considering. I could tell from her tone of voice that counted in my favour. 'I think perhaps we might be able to have that cup of tea some time. Give me a ring anyhow when you get up here.'

This was the most promising offer yet. She hadn't given me a meeting place or time, but she was definitely relenting.

By chance, the day I drove out to Wellington was 26 January, Australia Day. A large American ute with full-sized Australian flags flying from either side of the cabin sped down the motorway beside me as I headed westwards. It was only one ute, but its bulky size and the flags gave it the air of a military convoy, unquestionable right on its side. Between the two flags was a giant plasma-screen television, tied down securely. Other cars passed with smaller flags waving, carefully attached to an aerial or side mirror. I felt like an outsider.

In Bathurst, where I stopped for coffee, the waitresses had Australian flags painted on their cheeks and a young man on a motor bike rode around and around the hot, mostly deserted streets, a flag wrapped around his shoulders. Then he stopped and sat in the heat outside the café, waiting for I don't know what. He looked very young and suddenly dispirited, a sad undertow to his patriotic aggression, as if he might at least suspect it was all foolish posturing.

Past Bathurst, early summer had been unusually rainy so the sides of the road waved with wild wheat and oats and the hillsides were covered with tussocky grasses a metre high, pale gold washed with green, the lovely unnameable colour just before ripeness. All the dams were full, glinting with water, and the creeks and occasional marshes were edged with bright green. Rolling hills unfolded one vista after another, seeming to invite the traveller ever onwards. After more than 400 kilometres the Wellington Valley opened before me as I crested a rise. I tried to imagine what it would be like to have been walking for days and to stand on that hill and see that you were nearly home, just another few hours' walk.

Another ten minutes' drive and I was at the cabin by the river. The water was flowing fast and muddy, the deepest I had seen it for several years. It had flowed past Wiradjuri babies being born and the bora initiation ceremonies and Oxley and the convicts and soldiers and the missionaries and my ancestors. I gazed at it for a few minutes, listening to the wind in the she-oaks making a low shir-shirring sound, like whispering just below comprehension, before turning to unpack.

First thing next morning I called in to talk to Lee. It was only nine o'clock but the heat was already bouncing off the road when I parked. Lee wasn't waiting on the veranda for me this time and, as it turned out, was asleep. He answered the door after a few minutes, tousled and sleepy-eyed, blinking at the bright world outside his dim little house, gradually remembering that he had agreed to see me. I said I would come back in half an hour when he was awake. I really only had a couple of questions, a few minutes of his time.

When I returned he had showered and shaved and was

back to his usual speed of a million miles an hour. We went straight into his kitchen, still bare and neat even after a sleep-in, and he poured us each a drink from the water purifier on the sideboard before we sat down at the formica table. No need for cautious standing and checking this time; we already had each other's measure.

I asked Lee about the present stage of the claim and he said it was still undergoing pre-registration tests. It had been going back and forth between the lawyer, Tietzel, the Native Title Tribunal and the claimants.

'Teitzel says in his experience with the other claims he's represented that this one has to be registered or something funny is going on. He said it can't be knocked on the head.'

'He's that certain?'

'Yep. He's done a few of these before where the wrong mob have had a go. There's no doubt Rose has rights, through the Stanleys, but seventy per cent of the rest have none.'

'So why did the government give the land to Rose's mob instead of listening to the Traditional Families?'

'You know about the town tip out on the Common?'

'Yes, on the road to Nanima.'

'It's been used for all sorts – not just town garbage – hospital waste, farm chemicals. Balmain and Leichhardt councils in Sydney used it for a few years as well. And some sewage. There's these three streams, water courses, that go through it – I can show you the maps – and it's only 400 metres or so from the river. I can show you. After rain, there's a lot of seepage into the river. And we get our water just two kilometres down from the tip.'

'Is that right?'

River pollution was important but didn't seem to be anything to do with my question. I was trying to stay on track here; I didn't want to give him anything more than polite interest.

'I could show you documents. You won't find them on the internet or anywhere else.' I nodded and he was out of the room and back with two folders, both at least ten centimetres thick, within a few seconds. 'Just a few bits and pieces on the tip.' He grinned.

He knew he was obsessive and was proud of it. He took out various papers showing non-compliance for various water-testing procedures by Wellington Council, some local newspaper clippings chronicling opposition to the tip, and one with an obscured letterhead. He picked up the last one.

He held it out for me to read but didn't let me hold it. It was dated 1997 and it contained a report with figures and graphs on the bacterial quality of the Macquarie River at various towns along its length tested over a period of time. 'Look at this.' He flicked through the pages. 'Here are the graphs for the other towns – Dubbo, Narromine. Zero faecal coliforms means drinking quality, up to 150 is okay for swimming, something like 450 for stock use – and here look, the graph for Wellington, 1700, then 1800, 1900.'

'And arrows pointing off the graph.'

I wrote down the name and identification number of the paper. I thought of the glass of water I had drunk in my cabin this morning and felt a bit queasy.

'Exactly. But you won't find this anywhere. Fell off the back of a friend's truck. I showed it to this government minister and he said, Lee, where the hell did you get that and I said never you mind, but I gave him a copy.' He put the paper away, looking pleased with himself.

'It must have changed since then, that was more than ten years ago.'

'Nothin's changed. What's changed? Tip is still there, water treatment plant still the same. It doesn't have facilities to treat this kind of pollution. I'll show you what the water from the tap is like.' He jumped up again and fetched a plastic bucket of brownish water from the front room. 'I got that from the tap yesterday.'

Well, it has been raining, I thought. Later I looked up the latest river quality data and found the faecal coliform count for the day of the brownish bucket of water was seventeen, a very long way from the data that fell off the back of a truck, but not zero either.

I took a deep breath. I had to get back on track or I would be here all day being swept along in his battles.

'This river pollution is really important, I mean everyone in the town needs to know if it still is the case, but it hasn't got anything to do with the battle over the Common, has it? I asked you about why the government gave the land to one lot when the other lot had shown they were the traditional owners.'

'Which lot do you think agreed to let the tip stay on the Common and keep quiet?'

Before I left, Lee took two calls on his mobile. One was from Violet Carr, Wayne's mother, complaining about how dirty the tap water was today, and the other was from Wayne, still in Sydney, about the upcoming registration determination. When Wayne heard I was there, he said, 'Look, the thing she has to understand about the tip, it's on that sacred site I was tellin' her about. Pine Hill.'

I remembered he had told me about Pine Hill when we talked in Erskineville, after I had stopped the tape and we were at his front door. Pine Hill was where Wandong (or Yandong), the son of Baiame and progenitor of the Wiradjuri lived. Pine Hill. The son of Baiame who brought into existence all the hills, Baron Rock too, and the rivers, had lived on that very hill. I knew that when Baiame slept he rolled over and the salt water covered his body. The moon and stars fell down and became embedded in his muddy flesh, white fossil crescents and star shapes, and I had found them in a dry gully when I was a child. Apparently one day in the future, Baiame will roll over again and the salt water will once more cover his body. I wondered whether it would wash away the jam tins and tomato sauce bottles, car chassis and disposable nappies sticking onto his son's skin.

I tried to ring Rose but there was no reply. I couldn't tell if I was relieved or not.

Later I looked through the *Wellington Times* clippings about the tip that Lee had given me – some of them written by Beryl O'Brien, a local journalist and second cousin of mine. There was opposition from Traditional Families, along with other locals, when the tip was first established on part of the Common in the mid eighties.

'What Rose is doing is against Aboriginal law,' Wayne is

reported as saying in the newspaper. 'Elders set rules under Aboriginal law. There's been no respect for our elders and decisions are being made without their consent.'

He also said they were concerned about the road that Rose had built on the Common, the location of the tip, illegal sewerage and the likelihood of pollution leaching into the river. The blockade lasted a week and resulted in the council agreeing to allow Wayne to address it on the Common issue. The Environmental Protection Agency was asked to inspect the tip, but it turned out pollution measurement devices were already in place there.

There was really nothing anyone could call evidence to link the decision to transfer the Common to Rose's committee to fears that if the Traditional Families had the Common, they would continue to kick up a stink about the tip and river pollution. Garbage disposal, sewerage and water quality are local council issues; land rights are a Federal and State issue and there is no piece of paper that links the two. There are only mutterings.

Back in Kings Cross the weeks slipped by. It felt like I was nearing the end of the story, but there was still Rose. I still wanted to ask Wayne why he was bothering with a Native Title claim when he knew Rose had freehold title to the Common, but I kept putting it off. When I finally did try to phone there was a message saying his number was no longer connected. I wondered if he had not been able to pay his bills or whether he had just moved on. I rang Joyce. It took a few days of phone calls before I found her at home and she told me

Wayne had moved back to Wellington. He was living in Short Street, up the road from the house where my Aunt Dorothy had lived with her husband and children.

He answered the phone immediately and didn't sound at all surprised to hear from me.

'How's Wellington?' I asked.

'It's my place, I'm home,' he said.

He sounded happy and relaxed. He had his grandchildren with him and they were settling in well.

'I've got one more question for you,' I said. 'I know we talked about all this, but I need you to clarify why you are continuing with the Native Title claim when it won't give any real rights over the Common because it's freehold now?'

'So everyone knows we were right in the first place. The Land Council, Native Title Services, the government – they will all have to admit we were right all along, the Traditional Families are the rightful custodians.'

Wayne simply wanted it admitted by all concerned that they had the inalienable right to the land, the right by Wiradjuri law for 40,000 years and acknowledged by Australian law since 1993, to say this land was theirs. And that Rose and her mob did not have the right. Well, Rose might but she hadn't gone about it according to Aboriginal law.

It must have stuck like a barbed spearhead in Wayne's side that Rose was sitting on the land that his ancestors, the most feared clan in the whole Wiradjuri nation, had defended for unwritten millennia.

'And there's other sacred sites. I can show you some if you like. Too hot now, but when it gets a bit cooler or early one mornin',' he said.

253

He kept on going before I could say anything. He was an orator in front of the assembly, he was going to have his say. He couldn't let it go; it would be like letting go of the only thread that connected him to his own soul.

'So, you want a moral victory then?'

'More than that. Once our claim is registered – and Teitzel says we can't fail, we have such a strong case – we will use it as a platform to ask why the wrong people were given the land. And why weren't we listened to. They all knew, we told 'em. We want to expose the way the so-called land rights system really works.'

'You want to attack the whole thing?'

'That's right. It's big. The way it works now, anyone can be on a local land council. It's a denial of Aboriginal tribal identity. It's forced assimilation.'

'So this is not just about ownership of the Common?'

'It's about the policies of relocatin' tribal people all over the place. There's nineteen different tribal groups in Dubbo and you see all the trouble they have there. It sets Aboriginal people against each other. Divide and rule. It's colonial policy.'

'What do you want to happen then?

'For a start, the land councils need to be replaced by tribal councils. Each tribe has its own council. And stop shifting people around all over the place, making it impossible for them to stay on their own land.'

'I think it's more ignorance than deliberate policy,' I defended.

'It's subliminal,' Wayne said. 'They don't admit it, but they don't really respect Aboriginal law.'

He went on to point out that all the other cultural groups

in Australia – Chinese, Vietnamese, Italians – were encouraged to practise their own language and cultures. Why wasn't the difference of separate Aboriginal nations recognised? He wanted to undo a system that, under the guise of land rights, was undoing the ancient rule of elders and dividing and ruining Aboriginal communities.

'It's going to take a while,' I said.

'That's all right. I'm not goin' anywhere. Everyone knows I'm not gunna give up on this.'

After the phone call I went downstairs to the café for a coffee. The young woman who brought it to my table was French so I chatted for a minute. The coffee smelled and tasted like memory, rich and addictive, and I sat back, at ease despite the strange restlessness Wayne's determination aroused. The street flowed with the sounds of different languages as it had ever since Europeans began disembarking from sailing ships and steamers down in the bay and walking up the steep steps to Kings Cross. Each language, each person, carried a different story. Sometimes I want to hear every one of them.

32

Sacred Sites

After weeks of phone calls, Tim had managed to pin Lee and Wayne down. They were going to show us some Wiradjuri sacred sites, traditional meeting places along the river and in the hills behind town. I had left it to Tim to set up. Simply by being male he had more clout with Lee and Wayne than I did, but he also shared their general suspicion of my reliance on books rather than the world in front of me. Even though I had met Lee and Wayne first and introduced them to Tim, I knew I was lucky to be allowed to come along. I stayed overnight in the cabin by the river so as to be up and ready to go when they were.

The Wellington Valley can be as cool and white-grassed as the high country on a clear autumn morning; I do remember numb fingertips, and frost crunching underfoot on the way to the backyard toilet when I was a child, but somehow I recall the Valley as continually hot. It was not cold now, just unseasonably cool. A breeze lifted my hair as I walked along the veranda outside the retirement units where I'd arranged to pick up Tim. The fresh morning air made it feel like another brighter, more lively place.

Tim was already inside, having a cup of tea with Mum. He got up to make me one while I took his place on Mum's right side where she could hear better. She couldn't make tea anymore; it wasn't safe for her to lift a jug of boiling water. Even drinking a cup of tea was a bit risky. I watched as she lifted the cup wobbling to her lips and then placed it wobbling back down in its saucer.

But she wanted to hear about our plans.

'Don't think they want a girl along,' I said to Mum, winking.

'You be careful now.'

'I'll be fine. They probably think I'll slow them down. I'll get to the top of that hill before any of them.'

After finishing the tea we left in my car. We collected Lee and then Wayne, and Tim got in the car with them while I drove along behind. I followed them to The Falls on the Macquarie River, which are not any kind of falls but rather a ford. No-one seems to know why it's called The Falls; perhaps someone heard it wrong once and it was repeated and gradually changed in everyone's minds.

We were out past the edge of town along a road that was gravel until fairly recently and still does peter off into dirt. It's the unknown side of town to me; I can't ever remember going out that way as a child. I realise it doesn't take much for a place to feel foreign to me. It seems contradictory that the early morning streets of Paris feel familiar, while a road on the other side of my home town can shimmer with strangeness.

When I pulled up and got out of the car I remembered the first time I came to The Falls, probably in my late twenties. It was a ferocious summer day, hot beyond the capacity of thought or will, and I had walked a short way along the river bank looking for somewhere to swim, before simply stopping in my tracks, stunned by the heat. I'd stood in silence. There were red river gums and she-oaks around me and sandy soil underfoot. I waited; sweaty skin, flies – and the promise that something would be revealed. The yearning for whatever it was took hold of me as it had before in the bush, the familiar pang of the moment before revelation. And then in a few more moments it had gone and I was left hot and desolate as always.

It wasn't going to happen today. We were about business. The river was muddy and there were dried-out car tracks backing and turning away from the ford. The men stood with their hands in their jacket pockets, looking at the ground and scratching patterns in the soil with the toes of their boots. They were waiting for me.

Corroborees were held here right up to the end of the nineteenth century, Wayne explained. I had read about this place but had not known where it was. He said his ancestors built a huge Baiame figure here from sand and soil, metres long, lying on the ground.

'It was made for initiation ceremonies. Re-built each year.'

'That was out at the bora ground, wasn't it? The Baiame figure?'

He looked at me. 'Nah, it was here.'

'Well, there was one at the bora ground too. That's what I've read in Henderson.'

Wayne ignored me. He took some photos out of his jacket pocket. He showed me three of them. They were pictures of men with painted bodies and feathers in their hair, copies of images taken at the last corroboree held here some time in the late 1870s.

'Women can't see the rest,' he said. He gazed at me intently, willing me to argue, I thought.

'Okay,' I said, and stepped back.

Wayne held the other photographs out to Tim who took them carefully. He was almost cradling them. I could see he felt honoured.

'I'll get him later and hold him down and make him tell me,' I joked.

'No, you won't,' Tim said.

He was terse and serious and I felt uncomfortable. I was only joking. Wayne and Lee took no notice of me. I looked around and tried to imagine flickering firelight and stamping feet and painted bodies in the ancient dark. I didn't feel anything. There was nothing here.

We got back in the cars and drove into town and across several streets to the junction of the Bell and Macquarie. We parked in the V between the rivers and got out. It was a stony, sandy strand. Wayne told us that a gigantic kangaroo was drawn here, not carved but made in outline with stones and rocks. It was created before a hunt, a kind of spell to bring hunting success. I wondered if it was made before every hunt or just sometimes when the hunters were desperate – surely a lot of work to do when you were hungry – but I didn't ask.

I can't remember why, and it could have been apropos of nothing, but Wayne suddenly started talking about the killing of 'unfit' children. 'If you were born with anything wrong with you, you were knocked on the head. Or if you couldn't learn or keep up, you were knocked on the head.' He gave me his intent look again.

'They couldn't carry anyone who couldn't carry themselves,' I said. 'Subsistence life.'

'Yeah,' he said. 'It's just the way it was. I'm just saying it like it was. Too old or crook, or a kid who couldn't keep up, knocked on the head.' He wasn't defending or accusing; he was almost dispassionate except that he still seemed to be trying to get a reaction. 'Knocked on the head,' he said again.

Some things are better now, I thought, but didn't say. And then Wayne said the words exactly as I'd thought them: 'Some things are better now.'

I nodded without looking at him.

For a few minutes we discussed whether we would go out to Pine Hill where the tip was, but Wayne wanted to take us out to Bushrangers Creek first. I said I had already been out to Pine Hill and so had Tim, so we all headed out along Bushrangers Creek road. We went up past the showground – the land that had belonged to our great-grandparents years ago – and past Kellys' house with all the truck and car bodies lying around and then into the bush. It still felt like the 'other way' home, still had its air of difference and slight danger.

We stopped just past the turn-off to Mount Arthur where the Aboriginal shanty settlement had been. I had a vague picture in my head of the tin houses being there during my early childhood, but later on when the shanties had disappeared I wondered if I had imagined them. Before Nanima, Wayne had lived there with his grandmother in one of the houses made of flattened honey tins. He showed us the spot; all that was left of his childhood home was a few bits of rusty battered tin. There was some fencing wire and a few cans lying around in the tussocky grass. The ground was stony, nothing much would grow here.

'When I was a kid I always wanted to live here in one of these houses,' Tim said suddenly.

Coming from anyone else it might have sounded pat-ronising, but I knew he meant it. His face had the glow of childhood yearning. Tim, with his thick Buddy Holly glasses, had been a curious, snowy-haired kid who lived in his own world. Tim hadn't wanted, still didn't want, what most other people want. Wayne looked at him and grinned.

I walked through the grass, kicking, finding scattered remains. I felt more connected to this place. People had lived here; I remembered them. Lee and I trailed around, picking up the odd tin to identify, golden syrup cans and sauce bottles, while Tim and Wayne talked, exchanging facts and lining up memories of their separate boyhoods.

Wayne was a bit edgy as well. Tim noticed it and men-tioned it to me later. We both thought it would have been in this place in the middle of his childhood that the sexual abuse had happened. It wasn't, but he didn't want to stay here long.

We headed up the road towards Mount Arthur. Wayne showed us a valley at right angles to the road and narrowing as it headed up into the bush before widening out into a kind of circular space. Like a birth canal, I thought. At the end was a large rock, almost lingam-shaped. Around it there were shoots of green nourished by run-off and better soil.

'Here,' said Wayne, 'is where children were brought in the night and given their star-name.'

'Really? A star-name! What was that? How did that work?'

'Their star-name – their star was pointed out to them and it was theirs. From when they were born. It was their star-name.'

'So they brought them here, little kids, in the dark?'

'Yeah.'

He looked around. He seemed sad suddenly, that strange almost pointless sadness that can wash through anyone at any time. It was a sunny morning, starting to warm up, a few centuries since the Europeans arrived thinking nothing much was going on here.

I felt a pang of envy. I would have liked to have been given a star-name.

I considered for a moment. Maybe I didn't know Wayne well enough to say it, but then I decided to try it. 'It's like a birth canal, this place – a womb and birth canal.'

Wayne flashed me a look of such amazed appreciation that I glowed foolishly.

'That's right,' he said.

He probably hadn't believed I'd got anything, and maybe I hadn't, but I could imagine children gazing at the night sky and the handing on of knowledge and the mystery of being in a vast universe.

'I want to come back here one time at night,' I said. 'Would that be all right?'

'Yeah, yeah.'

I imagined finding my star and then wondered if it would have to be pointed out to me by someone else. I wouldn't be

game to come along on my own anyway. Tim might come
with me. He loved the night sky; he studied astronomy and
the physics of night light and had painted the dark many
times. It was not blackness to him, but alive with absorbed
and reflected light.

We drove a bit further out along Bushrangers Creek
towards the farm and then in through a gate with a notice saying trespassers will be prosecuted. We jolted along a washed
out road then got out to clamber up Irribung as Wayne called
it. The ground was rocky underfoot and we had to watch
our step. From the top, near the steel girders of a commu-
nications tower, we could see Wellington lying seemingly
peaceful below and then as far as the eye could see, the patch-
work of farmland, and in the far distance, blue hills. Wayne
pointed out the Warrumbungle Ranges, faintly blue in the far
distance.

He said that you could see Baiame's footprints from up here
but I couldn't see anything. It didn't really matter. We were
on top of a high hill and the wind was blowing through us. I
felt my rib cage expand and my bones lighten with the pecu-
liar joy of high places. We all stood looking over Wiradjuri
country, breathing the cool air and feeling the wide sky.

33

What Happens in Wellington

It was only a few weeks later, February, when I was back up in Wellington. It was very hot and dry again, the beginning of another year of drought. The few good rainfalls the previous year had run into the gullies and evaporated and there was a feeling that the dry spell was going to last for months.

At my mother's place I knocked on the door, but she didn't answer. I let myself in. She was sleeping in her chair curled to one side, saliva dribbling a little from her lips. Cushions had been pushed down one side of the chair but she had slid forward and down, her back curled like a foetus. The ordinary pain of her mortality slid sharply into me, a fish hook of loss, and I wanted to shake her, wake her and make her stand up and stride briskly out the door. I carefully took a hanky out of her pocket.

'Hallo, Mum. I'm here.'

She woke easily and I dabbed the corner of her mouth and then made a cup of tea. Afterwards I watered the petunias and pansies that my younger sister, Mary, had planted for her in large blue pots. They were drooping in the dry heat.

In the afternoon I went to the *Wellington Times* office to check the articles Lee and Wayne had mentioned. They both told their stories with such conviction that I was inclined to believe them without question, but I still needed to have printed versions. I stepped into the office and both felt and heard the noisy air-conditioning. There was a friendly-looking blonde woman behind the counter.

'Oh, hello. You're Terry's sister, aren't you?'

I nodded, incredulous, as the middle-aged woman dissolved into the girl who had lived over the road from my grandmother. My brother had played cricket with her brother. In this town, more than I had ever thought, I was not just recognisable as someone's sister, cousin, daughter, neighbour, niece, but I, in turn, recognised sisters, cousins, nieces, children. I fitted into the ordinary neighbourly layers of history and connection. I realised with some surprise that it gave me pleasure.

She photocopied the articles for me and I answered her questions about the family. We didn't know each other, we had not even played together as children, but we knew each other's families in detail.

As I stepped back into the street, the heat hit with the same force as the sudden blast on opening an oven door.

'Hot enough for you?' said the man coming in.

'Just about,' I said.

I headed down to the swimming pool to do some laps. Despite the heat and the fact that it was still school holidays, there was only a handful of people there, mostly Aboriginal kids. It had been that way for a few years now. When I was a child in the sixties, the pool was always packed all summer. Perhaps the white families all had air-conditioning and their own swimming pools now.

I did my laps slowly and felt nervous when a group of Aboriginal kids moved into the lane I was using. There were about six or seven of them, teenagers, bigger than I am, lazily throwing a ball between themselves. They had started off on the other side of the pool but when I finished one of my slow laps, there they were in my lane. I couldn't tell if it was deliberate or not. My dogged, ungainly, middle-aged lapping could easily have inspired the desire to disrupt – it would only be natural. I swam around them.

On the next lap they had spread out into two lanes. I caught my breath, splashed towards them, and then swam around them again. Their gaze followed my trajectory and when I reached the end there was a burst of laughter – which may have had nothing to do with me. It was probably just the drift of their ball throwing and their conversation that led them across the pool. Any threat was probably in my imagination. That's what happens in Wellington.

When I arrived back at my mother's, still with wet hair, I phoned Rose for the third time since I'd arrived. By now I thought I was just being dutiful and was hoping she wouldn't be home. She answered just as I was about to hang up. With only a brief to and fro, she agreed to see me for tea at ten thirty the next morning.

'I'll bring the cake,' I said, trying to hide my exultation. So, I had wanted to talk to her after all.

'Buy me some Madeira cake,' said Rose.

'Madeira cake? Okay then, I'll see what I can find.'

After a few moments more of reassuring checks about the time and how to find her, I put the receiver down.

'She wants Madeira cake,' I said to my mother.

'Then you had better go and find some,' she said.

I tried Kimbell's Bakery next to the lane Aunt Millie ran down to escape the police. It was closed. Then Woolworths – it had no Madeira cake. I started to drive back to the cabin. No, she had asked for Madeira, it was the least I could do. I stopped the car, turned around and drove to the ugly Bi-Lo where I found two types of Madeira, one with pink icing and one with lemon. I chose the lemon.

I set the alarm and next morning before dawn hauled myself groggily out of bed. It was going to be a scorcher. I planned to climb the hill out on Pete's farm to look down on the bora ground before I visited Rose, which meant the car would be sitting out in the blinding heat quietly turning itself into a furnace. I put the cake in an Esky with an icepack and a bottle of water.

It was still before 6.30 am. I drove past the farm house without stopping. I had rung Pete the day before and told him I would tip-toe in and out before the heat and without waking anyone. There was a gate and a ramp just as I remembered, then a ramp with a barrier across which I didn't recall. It didn't seem I'd driven far enough, but I didn't like to move the barrier.

I parked the car. The sacred hill rose to my right, but I was unsure whether it was the one overlooking the bora ground. Perhaps there was another one further around? I don't know whether it was the early morning giving me the feeling of acting secretively, but I started to feel unsure. Should I be doing this at all? Climbing sacred hills? And worse, trying to see a male initiation site? But that was 200 years ago. It was just a paddock along a river bank now. And none of the Wiradjuri I'd met knew or seemed greatly concerned about where it was anymore. Did that make any difference? I sat, arguing the case silently.

The sky was getting lighter. If I was going to do it I should start climbing. I jumped out of the car and headed up the hill. Immediately I thought I should turn back; the dried grass was thigh high, a veritable garden of snake nests, and I was foolishly dressed in shorts and thongs. It was my mother's fiercest rule in summer: never walk through long grass and absolutely never ever without shoes and long trousers. I could only hope the snakes were still asleep. My eyes scanned the ground as I tried to pick my way through, walking on rocks and avoiding the thickest grass.

I clambered up alongside a fence for a while, my legs stretching out from rock to rock, then I climbed through it, avoiding the barbed wire along the top by holding it carefully up with one hand. On the other side I set off at a diagonal across and up the hill, high-stepping like an anxious horse through the long grass when I couldn't go around it and feeling relieved each time I gained a rocky platform. I kept climbing steeply upwards for half an hour, the air still cool on my face.

I stopped two or three times then veered around the high rocks where Tim had said the churinga stone had been found. I could suddenly see another high hill, which had been hidden behind the first and looked very similar to it. I looked down towards the river to where it looped away behind the second hill. Below, not far from the river, was a derelict house I had passed with Tim in the car; I was obviously no further along than I had been that day months ago. Against my nature I had got up before dawn and climbed a steep hill, disobeying my mother and risking my life walking among snakes and I was on the wrong bloody hill.

If I believed in such things I would say the ancient spirits were showing me who was in charge. Whatever it was, I realised I didn't actually care. I was even vaguely grateful. I had been saved from seeing what I shouldn't. I sat down on a rock to look back over the landscape.

Although it was only twenty kilometres away as the crow flies from the farm where I spent my childhood, the land here was quite different. The hills were higher and steeper and overlapping each other into the distance, creating a landscape of drama and promise, especially as the first rays of sun hit the hill on the other side with a glancing wedge of light. I thought of Baron Rock behind the farm, the place where something might be discovered. I was up high with the eaglehawks again. The long grass glowed golden like a wheat field in a Sisley painting, a rich soft yellow, brightly lit. All around and over the broad arrow of gold lay the dreaming atmosphere of the bush, its unfathomable mystery. Native pines and eucalypts gathered on the hillsides, silvery grey and dark grey boulders leaned like dolmens, still and silent. It was so beautiful it hurt, and so secretive that I felt rebellious.

This place would not tell what it knew, not in a hundred years, but one day, I would come and sit and wait endlessly until it yielded.

34

Country Rose

Later in the morning, when the rest of the world was awake and going about its business, I headed out to the Common. It was quiet, not another car on the road. Lee had given me directions for finding Rose the day before – turn right through Nanima at the school, drive over the grid, then follow the side of the hill around until I saw the tin humpy. As I coasted down the hill into Nanima the settlement looked peaceful, almost asleep in the already hot sun. Although it was past the hour school went in, there were still a couple of kids straggling into the schoolyard. The first day back but summer and the river still beckoned. They looked at me, already bored. What was I doing here?

I bumped over the grid and was on the Common at last. I slowed down, feeling as if some revelatory moment ought to happen. I couldn't think what, but after all this time, some epiphany should arrive. The land was different again here; rolling hills sloping down to river flats dotted with eucalypts and wattles, and closer to the river, willows and she-oaks. The yellow grasses were thick and long, native rye with green splashes of exotic clover and lucerne, evidence of dark river loam and a bit of moisture in the soil. It probably didn't look much different from the way it looked in 1867 when my great-great-great-grandfather Patrick Reidy and his Town Common Committee first commandeered it.

I saw a low shack made of tin in a fenced paddock and pulled over. A woman appeared in the shade of the trees around the shack and waved me on, indicating that I follow the road as it turned up the hill. I continued on around the back to a wide gate and parked in the small shade of a sapling gum. The woman opened the gate and waited under the overhanging peppertree as I got out of the car with my books and papers. I went around to the boot, got the cake out of the Esky then walked towards her. It seemed perfectly ordinary and comfortable to be meeting Rose at last.

We looked at each other, a moment of mutual appraisal, then said each other's names. Just to be sure. In those first few moments with her, I had an overwhelming impression, not of ego or self-aggrandisement, but of a great weariness. She was only a few years older than me, but she seemed utterly worn. She was short and stocky, her facial features heavy, wide nose and full lips, dark brown skin and beautiful thick dark hair, pinned up because of the heat I supposed. I wondered what she saw – a freckle-faced white woman, her skin flushed red and shiny, an eager, inquisitive look in her eye?

I handed her the cake, explaining that I hadn't known what kind of Madeira to buy. She said there was only one kind. I said the Bi-Lo had one with pink icing and one with lemon and she said she didn't eat icing anyway. Cake talk took us across the yard so that I had only an impression of sunburnt grass underfoot and gum saplings and fruit trees around us. I stood in the violent blinding heat outside the open door of the tin shack waiting to be invited in before realising I was expected to simply walk in. I stepped through ahead of Rose.

The quality of the heat changed immediately, becoming heavy and suffocating under the low corrugated iron roof and walls. The light was dim at first, coming in through a window facing towards the river flats, but I could see the room was made of bits and pieces of fibro and building board as well as tin. Hessian was pinned over part of the roof to make a ceiling, and there were wheat bags here and there on the floor. There were a table and chairs, a homemade side bench crowded with tins, food cartons and an electric jug and toaster, and a sink on brick pylons. By the sink, a garden tap came out of the earthen floor, and on the other side of the room a row of tools lay neatly on a shelf under the window. I thought of the hippy shack with the tarpaulin roof where I once lived as a young woman. Instead of pictures of mandalas and Indian gurus, there was a framed picture of a young and beautiful Elvis Presley in the corner. The shack had the same look of practical making-do with what could be found – except for a magnificent collection of Royal Doulton on shelves across one wall. It was the largest collection I had ever seen outside a shop: cups and saucers, a teapot, jugs, tureens, bowls, dinner plates, bread-and-butter plates, serving dishes; all roses and gilt and all covered in dust. I thought about how much it must have cost.

'My mum has a cup and saucer of that pattern,' I said.

'I fell in love with Country Rose when I was sixteen. I first saw it when I went to Sydney.'

I hadn't known that's what the pattern was called but I nodded knowledgeably. I wondered if she liked it because of the name.

'It's lovely.' I said. 'Mum likes nice cups and saucers too, so we buy them, one at a time, for her birthday and Christmases.' I was letting her know I was aware how much Royal Doulton cost and where the hell did she get the money.

'My husband bought them for me. One at a time. Over twenty years.' She was letting me know no-one could accuse her of spending funding grants on pricey china. There are things you don't mention aloud if you are just sitting down to have a cup of tea with someone, but if you both know the rules you can cover a fair bit of ground anyway.

'It's great that he knows what you like. And that he gives it to you.'

'I've got a good bloke. I'm one of the lucky ones. He's a good man.'

Her voice was stronger, stating a rare appreciation. I remembered that Gaynor and Joyce both thought her husband was aggressive, and I realised perhaps he was only defending Rose.

'I've got a good one too,' I offered.

She flashed me a look, both of us glad to have someone to share our good fortune with.

'So he's not here at the moment?'

'He lives in town now. He stayed out here for a while, fixed lots of things, but if you're not used to it, it's too hard to live like this. I grew up like this. We had to bucket all the water from the river. I've got this tap now.'

I stood with her by the sink as she bent down to fill the kettle from the tap coming out of the ground. 'When I was a kid we didn't have running water either,' I offered. 'Just the tank outside. Then when I was about twelve, Dad put a tap in the kitchen. Only cold water though. Never any hot. Except for the chip heater in the bathroom, but we hardly ever used the bath because of the drought.'

'Here. You take this knife and plate and cut up the cake.'

I cleared a space on the table and cut a slice for each of us. Rose brought the tea to the table, mine in a mug, hers in a gigantic glass tankard with five tea bags still dangling. No Royal Doulton for us. As Rose sat down she looked even more tired and her breath wheezed.

'A bit of asthma from the summer grass?' I said.

'Dunno. A bit of emphysema, I reckon. Gave up smoking three or four months ago.'

Shit! She really wasn't well. I wondered if I should be doing this.

'That's no good.'

Rose shrugged.

'So you live in Sydney these days?' she asked.

'Yes. I've been there for about three years. Before that I was in the Blue Mountains. I haven't lived in Wellington since I was eighteen. I like the country, but . . .' I didn't want to say not much cultural life out here, so I changed tack. 'It's a bit quiet for me.'

'No cultural life here. We're lucky if we get a play every three years.'

I nodded. I didn't have her measure but she certainly had mine, despite looking and sounding as if she'd had the stuffing knocked out of her.

'So, you grew up in this house?'

'It was my grandmother's house. We lived across the road.'

'Your grandmother was Tillie Bell?'

'Yeah. Whereabouts in Sydney do you live?'

'Kings Cross.'

'Oh, I used to work near there,' Rose exclaimed, showing the first sign of liveliness. 'Billyard Avenue. I was a mother's help in one of those big houses there.' She mentioned the name of a well-known Sydney family. 'The older son is a Park Avenue lawyer now. New York.'

'Better not say anything about him then?'

She grinned.

'So you went to Sydney when you were sixteen?'

'I fell in love with Sydney. Well, I was a bit lonely at first, but then I found a job as a nurse's aide and made lots of friends. I loved walking around Sydney. And I liked looking after old people. Then I was the mother's help at Billyard Avenue, then a nurse's aide again, then a nursing domestic.'

'Why did you leave?'

'It was getting expensive to live in Sydney and in 1986 we came up to Wellington for a bit of a break and decided to stay. We rented a house on a farm out on the Yeovil Road.'

'Really? That's where our farm was. Out towards Yeovil. Did you turn off at Fingerpost?'

'No, we kept going. Opposite Bishop's property'

'That would be Curra Creek. I was at Suntop school so we had school sports with Curra Creek.'

'Oh yeah. Curra Creek. It was good out there. Best nine years of my life. We had a beautiful garden. You shoulda seen our garden.'

'You're a good gardener?'

'We both are. My husband does the digging, I do the weeding.'

We were establishing our ground, checking that we really were locals. We knew this place, both of us. We knew who owned what property along a road that only a handful of people knew or cared about.

'So what started it all then? I mean, why did you get up one morning and decide you wanted to claim back the Common?'

'Well, it started with getting up one morning and reading the *Wellington Times*.' Her tone was dry, ironic.

'As you do,' I said.

'As you do.' She grinned again. We both got it, the mundane recording of country town life. 'And the headline said "The Common Up For Grabs". I thought, what's this? And I read on and it said the government was considering options for various bits of Crown land, and the Wellington Common was one of them. And I thought, they can't do that, that's our land.'

'So, when was that?'

'Late eighties, I think. I've been going on this a lot longer than the thirteen years they say in the papers. I wrote to the premier, who was it then? I said, give it to us.'

'That was the Town Common Committee?'

'Well, it didn't exist right away, but then we had the committee and we put a . . .' She seemed to have lost the thread. She sat leaning on one elbow, her tankard of tea in the other hand, eyes unfocused, drifting as if she had forgotten there was a sentence to finish.

'A claim, a land rights claim,' I suggested.

'That's what I was looking for.' She didn't seem bothered by her sudden vagueness, as if it was something she accepted. She continued on wearily. 'We put a land rights claim in to the New South Wales government in 1991 and then Eddie Mabo came along. We hadn't heard of him before, he was from the islands, you know, and three months later we put in our Native Title claim. The first one after Eddie Mabo.'

I had heard it all already but hearing it from Rose and seeing her great weariness I was beginning to feel some shame. I shouldn't have judged against her on the strength of other people's stories. And I hadn't confessed that I had arrived already implicated, aligned with the other side. Neither of us had even mentioned the other side yet.

'So what has kept you going all this time?'

She looked suddenly much more weary, almost beaten. She shrugged and grimaced as if she had actually been defeated. 'Just the land,' she said. 'It kept me going. The land.'

It was there outside the tin hut. The land all around us. Just river flats and low hills, soil and rye grass and clover and Bathurst burrs and gum trees. It was real and ordinary like earth anywhere, but it was also history and personal memory and identity as much for Rose as anyone else.

'So why did you leave here in the first place? You just wanted to go to Sydney? The bright lights?'

She leaned back and put her tea down. She was wearing a loose, ochre-coloured cotton dress and every now and then as we talked she leaned back and sighed in the heat and lifted her breasts with both hands to let the air under them. The unselfconsciousness of the breast-lifting rendered it a normal movement – of course you would lift heavy breasts in the heat to let the air cool and dry the sweat. We both sat there, a damp gleam coating our bodies, our only exertion drinking tea and cutting cake. Rose leaned forward again.

'We were moved off the Common. I was born here and I was thrown off. Certain people who said they were elders had something to do with that.' Her voice had an edge to it suddenly. 'People at Nanima who were the eyes and hands of the police and the government. And then they turn around a few years later and want your respect. Huh,' she scoffed bitterly.

I waited. It looked like she might tell me her version of where all the conflict had come from. She sat there drinking her tea then looked up. 'Anyway, I'll tell you more about it another time. We're just having a cup of tea today.'

'Okay, so you moved into Nanima after you were kicked off the Common?'

'Other people did. And some went into town. We went out to Mumbil. My dad got a job on the dam.'

Mumbil was a small village that housed workers on Burrendong Dam, built during the sixties on the Macquarie River upstream from Wellington to regulate floods and provide a steady water supply. It drowned some of the historic gold-mining and Aboriginal sites, and Joyce and Lee both said the local fish and mussels disappeared because they couldn't live in the cold water released from the dam.

'One day my mother went to Sydney to visit my sister, she was in hospital. And then my mother suddenly had a heart attack and died. And the next day my sister died. A week later my grandmother died.'

'That's terrible.' I flushed, feeling as inadequate as I ever had.

She was sitting heavily, and didn't respond. There was something damaged about her. She must have been only fourteen or fifteen when she lost her mother, sister and grandmother. The fish hook twisted a little.

'How old was your mum when she died?' I asked.

'She was fifty-six. All my life I have been frightened of turning fifty-six. I thought I wouldn't get past it myself.' Her lips started to tremble and tears shone in her eyes. 'When I was coming up to it, I was terrified. I was so scared. I thought I was going to die. I thought . . .' Her mouth wobbled uncontrollably and she stopped speaking.

'I know, that happens,' I said uselessly.

'I was so scared,' she said again, her voice soft and shaky. Her mouth slipped. She tried to hold it together but her whole face wavered then crumpled and she started to cry.

I sat awkwardly in the heat, unnerved. I put my cup of tea down. It wasn't that I was unused to tears, old sorrows often spring unexpectedly in life writing classes. But Rose's tears came from mortal terror, nothing to do with what I had come to ask her about. It wasn't any of my business. She sat at the table, her soft sturdy body shaking. I put my hand on her shoulder.

'Well, you've made it through. You're still here.'

My heart was thumping too loudly to think. Of course it was my business. Fear of non-existence is the dark thread connecting us all; tugging gently or fiercely, it is always there under each day.

She nodded, still crying. 'I was so frightened.'

She stared for a moment, directly ahead, then straightened and stood up heavily. Her facial muscles were still trembling and her skin was wet. She wiped the tears away with the back of her hand. 'That's what happens when you start stirring up memories. You get sentimental.'

She knew it wasn't sentiment. It was the heart knowing for certain that it would stop beating and that the whole shimmering world would disappear completely and forever, but who could say that over a cup of tea? The world was only solid while we believed it was. I took my hand away.

'But you're here now. On this beautiful piece of land. You have succeeded in what you set out to do.'

'I think it might have nearly done me in. The conflict.'

That was the second time she had brought it up. I decided to plunge in. 'I've heard a few things about that, the conflict. I've read some things. People have told me all sorts of things.'

Rose sat down again, heavily.

'There were people, are people, going around saying they are elders. Wanting you to respect them.'

'And you didn't think they deserved respect?'

'People treat you badly, treat your family badly. They get you thrown off your land, they break up your community – and then twenty years later they say they're elders and you should respect them. Sorry, I can't do that.' Her voice was flat and scathing.

So that's what it was about. An old wound that had never healed. She still hadn't named any names though. She was being justifiably careful.

'So the conflict between the two sides really started back in the sixties when your family was thrown off the Common?'

'It was already like that. Bill Riley, horrible man. He ran Nanima. He was a standover man.' She flashed me a look, knowing she had given me something. 'I know you talked to him all those years ago. You said in that first phone call. That's why I wouldn't talk to you then.'

Other people on the Traditional Families side had said the same thing about Bill Riley, but I had nothing against him. He had helped me with some good stories.

'I know, other people have said. But you know, he was nice to me.'

'Of course he was nice to you. A young woman writer, wanting to know about Aboriginal life? Of course he was nice to you.'

'So why did Bill Riley want you off the Common in the first place?'

Rose gave me another look that said, can't you work that one out. 'Because on the Common we were outside his jurisdiction,' she said flatly. 'He wanted everyone living at Nanima so he could have us under his rule.'

'So you reckon it was about personal power?' King of the castle, I suddenly thought.

'And there's Joycie Williams. Says she's an elder. She went round thinking she was better than everyone else, looking down her nose at us. Now Joycie says she's an elder and we have to look up to her. No thank you. I couldn't do that. No-one could do that and keep their dignity.'

I felt acutely uncomfortable and didn't know what to say. I liked Joyce and felt loyal to her, not to mention that I might be related. I didn't like the way Rose said 'Joycie', the tone of contempt. But this was Rose's side of the story and it had been the reason for the years of fighting over a few hectares of land and the splitting of the Aboriginal community. None of the story would have happened without her side of it. It was her reality and she felt hurt and angry and worn out. I had to listen.

'So what did Joyce do?'

'Thought she was better than us. Driving her car past us. Not stopping for nobody. Horrible woman.'

'Why would she do that?'

'Thought she was too good for Aboriginal people.'

'But she *is* Aboriginal.'

Rose made a scoffing sound. 'Joycie'd drive past her own grandchildren. Horrible woman. Her and her brother.'

'Why though?'

'She thought she was above us. Because Joycie was married to a white man.'

I knew Rose's husband was a white Englishman so that couldn't be the real reason for her dislike of Joyce. Later Joyce retorted her husband wasn't white. I realised I didn't want to hear any more. The conflict between Rose's mob and Joyce's mob was an antagonism born out of ill-considered government policy, but the conflict had become personal, a series of slights and hurts and insults built up over the years like a nasty midden. The midden wasn't the cause, it was the result. Grubbing through it only distorted the real issues of Native Title and Land Rights and gave ammunition to those who would deny them respect and acknowledgement.

Rose's family and many of the families on the Common were there because the Aboriginal Protection Board had closed their reserves and dispersed them to other places. They had nowhere to go and had ended up on local Wiradjuri land and were treated like interlopers. It was the same everywhere in the world, I thought; the newcomers are always resented through no fault of their own.

The forced relocation of Aborigines had happened because the government didn't know or care who belonged where, but for Rose, it was about feeling belittled where she was born. She and her family were made to feel like outsiders. And then she had lost her mother and her sister and her grandmother all within a week. Life had to feel fragile. She couldn't care less about proving a continuous connection back to white settlement; she just wanted to be on the land where she was born, back where she'd lived as a child when everyone was still alive.

I started gathering up my things. 'Can I just ask about the future – what you plan to do here? Then I'll leave you alone.'

'Yeah, I do need to get on with some watering.'

Rose cut herself another piece of Madeira. She had eaten three-quarters of the cake as we talked – and finished it off completely before we were done – carefully cutting the icing off each slice and putting it on the side of her plate. She told me about the work she had done so far, the trees she had planted, the restoration of the humpy and then her plans for a village – a whole village – on the Common, and a Cultural Centre, which Aborigines and non-Aborigines could come to from all over Australia. She said it would cost about three million dollars, although later she said, with all the things she had planned, she wouldn't have much change out of twenty million.

'You'd better buy a Lotto,' I said. From what I had read in various articles, there was no funding available from either State or Federal governments now that the land was freehold.

She smiled tiredly. 'There's a few places we can ask. And I want to build a Keeping Place. The Australian Museum in Sydney, they have some of our stuff. They would give that back to us if we had a Keeping Place.'

I hadn't asked about anything much on my list of questions: the town tip on the other side of the Common on Pine Hill; or the Traditional Families' plans for the same kind of cultural centre and Keeping Place at the old convict site; or the accusation of misappropriation of government funds; or the taunts that she had done it all for the money and would sell the land in five years' time so she and her committee could make a killing. These were all serious matters but I felt constrained.

Thinking about it now, I can understand why the mediation judge, 'the skinny sort of a little fella', didn't press Rose when she cried. Despite being a sturdy-looking woman, intelligent and perceptive, she had the air of a wounded, tired child who didn't want to be hurt anymore. Perhaps it was manipulative, as Wayne said, but I didn't think so. If it was, it was unconscious, and I didn't want to be the one who tested it.

Rose and I stood up and I cast another look around the little hut. There was a lean-to off the main room, a bedroom by the look of it, and another door, opening, I guessed, to a bathroom. I would have liked a proper look around but it's not what you do when you have a cup of tea. We went outside into the blinding heat and light, several degrees hotter than when we went in. It must have been forty-five degrees, the kind of heat that literally stops you in your tracks.

Ahead was a small portable building I hadn't noticed as I came in.

'The committee office,' Rose explained. Then she pointed out a smart-looking car under a carport next to the office. 'I bought that when they let me go at the hospital after thirteen years. Twenty thousand dollars I got, so I bought that car.' She was obviously well aware of what Joyce and Wayne were saying about her – and what might have flickered through my mind.

We walked slowly in that dream-like state extreme heat induces. When we reached the gate by the peppertree, I made one last effort to ask a question about her real intentions, her real motivation.

'So, do you reckon you will stay here long?'

'I'll leave here in a pine box,' she said, quick as a flash.

I nodded. So she wasn't going to sell the land, or at least didn't want anyone to think she would.

Or she didn't think she had long to go. So weary, leaning on the gate post.

'Then I'll come back and sit in one of them trees. Top of that gum tree.'

'What as?' I asked. I thought of the Wiradjuri totems, eaglehawk and crow.

'An eaglehawk.'

'Oh, yes, eaglehawks. I like them. I don't like crows.'

When I was a child standing on top of Baron Rock, I saw an eaglehawk hovering only a few metres away, watching intensely and waiting, its wings a blur.

'Crows are all right, I don't mind them. But the eaglehawk is powerful, majestic. He flies up so high, he's detached from everything. With his bird's-eye view of the world from so far up, so detached, he must have some wisdom about all this, eh?'

She looked at me directly. There was such longing in her eyes and voice that I felt disturbed. It wasn't simply poetic fancy, it was something she wanted very soon. She was utterly worn out; she'd had enough of all this.

'Yep, he must,' I said.

Things were never simple enough to take sides. Perhaps she did not have incontestable right to this land by Wiradjuri law, and Wayne and Joyce had every right to object, but in her heart, this was her place.

Rose closed the gate behind me and I walked back to my car. Within a few minutes I had left the Common but I was still on Wiradjuri land. I'd still be on Wiradjuri land if I drove in any direction for hundreds of kilometres – east to the Blue Mountains, west to Wagga Wagga, south to the Murrumbidgee River, north to Gilgandra. It had always been Wiradjuri land, but one day soon, the written law would acknowledge it.

From the top of Pine Hill, Wellington came into view. It looked peaceful and pretty, the streets regular and tree-lined, the wheat silos rising in the centre like a temple compound on the railway line. The rivers made two long protective arms, the hills on the other side – Moreebna and Irribung and Durra – formed a solid bush-covered backdrop. I couldn't see the footstep of Baiame, but that was only because I didn't know what to look for. The town looked the same as it always had.

35

Native Title

The year is nearly done. It is already the next summer since I talked to Rose and I am sitting on the wide country veranda of a house my brothers and sisters and I have rented in Wellington so that we can spend Christmas with our mother. After William Yarnold and Ann Smith were condemned to exile and sent across the wide ocean in a stinking convict hold, after Patrick Reidy fled starvation, after Pieter Müller left his safe cold village and after all of them trudged out into this stolen land to transplant themselves in a strange dry soil, not one of our generation owns a house in Wellington.

The house we have rented was built nearly a century ago, with various rooms added on over the years so it has a labyrinth of original rooms with tin-pressed ceilings joined onto a mid-twentieth-century rumpus room with glass doors and air-conditioning. There is a large beautiful garden with native eucalypts and bottlebrush and wattle growing alongside exotic lilies, gardenias and azaleas, and pretty pathways and a swimming pool. Our mother tells us that her father, a master painter, used to work for the architect who built and lived in this house and she is sure her father painted it at one time, maybe in the 1930s.

Today, eighty or so years later, there are grandchildren and great grandchildren and new bikes and wrapping paper and a strange blinking purple Christmas tree that came with the house. Inside, near the blinking tree, my younger son is reading Barack Obama's *Dreams of My Father* to my mother. It has taken an age to take her to the chair with her walking frame and she will only make the effort of getting up again to go to the lunch table. She is very frail, her skin covered in bruises from just the pressure of hands and she cannot sit upright without the help of cushions. I like seeing them together, the young man in the morning of his life, reading, and the old woman, nearly ninety, head leaning forward as she listens intently, both of them absorbed in the politics and the poetic writing.

It is the end of a long year of drought, but yesterday, Christmas Day, 'good steady rain' started to fall. It is still falling and it feels like a blessing even to those of us, most of us, who have lost the religion and God we were brought up with. We all remember the even longer drought of the sixties and so now we spend hours at a time sitting on the veranda, gazing at the silvery curtain of rain falling, falling, each of us feeling the joy of the parched soil drinking it in. Our memories float in the washed air; the farm, the old house, our father gone, our mother nearing her end – we all know, though we don't say, that it will be our last Christmas with her – all of us still children in ourselves.

Suddenly, my youngest brother, Terry, comes out through the gauze door onto the veranda carrying a copy of the *Wellington Times*. He shows me the front page. There is a large photo of Joyce and Wayne and his mother, Violet, smiling broadly under the heading 'Land Reclaimed'. I look up at my brother and he grins.

'They've done it!' I exclaim. 'After all this time! I didn't believe it would happen.' I feel elated and can't help smiling but then I realise I'm a bit disappointed that no-one has rung and told me. I know I don't matter in this at all, but I've been taking it fairly personally.

I ring Wayne and a child answers the telephone. She says Wayne is outside fixing up the car. I hear her calling out my name but his reply is indistinguishable. The child comes back and asks if I can ring back in half an hour.

This time Wayne answers.

'Still got to fix the car after all this?' I say.

'Yep,' he says. 'Life goes on.'

'I just saw it in the paper.'

'Isn't it bloody wonderful! That photo was taken out on the Common.'

'I thought it must have been. You all look pretty pleased. Best Christmas present ever.' I wonder if it's jarring to link it to Christmas but Wayne agrees.

'I didn't think it would ever happen,' I add.

'Yeah. I knew it would though. I wasn't ever goin' to give up. Not ever. I got the news a few days ago, my birthday actually. I thought Teitzel – he rang me – must have been kiddin' me at first. Thought it was the best birthday ever. Everything just happening the way I dreamed.'

'It's fantastic. And now the rain has come too.' I am not really changing the subject.

'Good steady rain,' he says. 'It's like a blessing.'

'Yes, that's what my dad used to say out on the farm. The land is happy too.'

'It's beautiful,' he says. 'Everything has happened just perfect.'

'I hope you've all celebrated.'

'Yeah, I'm having a few days off, but then I'll keep going. There's still a lot to do. It's only the beginning for my people.'

Afterwards I sit back on the veranda. I remember Rose and wonder how she is feeling. I hope she is with her family and I hope no-one is waving the newspaper headlines in front of her. On this rainy day when the grass and trees and red soil are drinking in great joyful gulps, I try to believe everyone might get along. I imagine for a moment Rose and Joyce and Wayne and all the rest, sitting down and putting aside their differences and past hurts and sorting it all out and everyone having their place. Even me, with my faint unproved trace of Wiradjuri, I would have a place. It was possible.

The rain falls on the gums and the azaleas and speckles the swimming pool. The city born-and-bred grandchildren are standing solemnly at the veranda's edge, a little awed by their parents' honouring of simple rain. I see a magpie hunching wetly under the swimming pool shelter. I suppose when the sun comes out and the rain is glistening on the leaves and grass, he will start to sing.

Epilogue

It is nearly Christmas again. Since last year when we all gathered on the veranda and watched the rain, my mother, Connie Miller, and Rose Chown have both died. My mother, determined and ironic until the end, died in Maranartha with my Buddhist brother on one side and me on the other. Rose died suddenly of a heart attack, alone, near her humpy on the Common. As the poet Yevgeny Yevtushenko said, 'Worlds in them have died.'

The rain that began at Christmas continued throughout the year and, although I have not seen it, I believe the Wellington Valley, with native grasses swaying on the hillsides and all the creeks flowing, is as beautiful as it has ever been. I have not returned there since my mother died, but I will. It's where the stories come from.

Acknowledgements

I would like to thank the Wiradjuri people who shared their knowledge and their memories with me so generously: Joyce Williams, Evelyn Powell, Wayne Carr and Rose Chown (now deceased). Without their open-hearted conversations I would not have been able to write this book. Thanks are due to Darren Ah See for speaking to me about Aboriginal Health issues. I offer thanks to local historian Lee Thurlow, to anthropologist Gaynor Macdonald, and to my brother, Tim Miller, for sharing their knowledge and joining in the search for the Wiradjuri story. I have tried to be faithful to what I heard and read. I hope I have represented everyone's memories and knowledge accurately and ask them to forgive any of my lapses. This is no more than my own version of the many stories I found.

Boundless thanks are due to Hilary M Carey and David A Roberts for extracts from the online version of *The Wellington Valley Project: letters and journals relating to the Church Missionary*

Society Mission to Wellington Valley NSW 1830–45, where I spent many addicted hours reading the missionaries' diaries and letters. Note, where different missionaries have spelled the same Wiradjuri name in different ways, I have kept Reverend Watson's spelling.

I would also like to acknowledge some of the many other sources that inform this story: *Wiradjuri Places, The Macquarie River Basin* by Peter Kabaila, 1998; *History of Wellington* by Robert Porter, 1906; *Wellington Valley, Its History and Progress 1817–1934* by WM Smith, 1934; *Ghosts of Burrendong* by Dale Edwards, 2008; *The Adventurous Memoirs of a Gold Diggeress 1841–1909* by Mary Ann Tyler, 1985; *The Glint of Gold* by Kerrin Look and Daniel Garvey, 1999; *They Came to a Valley* by DI McDonald, Wellington, 1968; *Initiation Ceremonies of Wiradjuri Tribes* by RH Matthews; and *Narrative of a Visit to the Australian Colonies* by J Backhouse. And a special acknowledgement to the Mitchell Library for *Observations on the Colony of New South Wales and Van Dieman's Land* by John Henderson, 1832; and *An Australian Language: the Wiradjuri Dialect* by J Günther, 1892.

And again, thanks to Gaynor Macdonald for her essay 'A Man's Wage for a Man's Work: equality and respect in Aboriginal working lives in NSW', 2004; for her books *Two Steps Forward, Three Steps Back: a Wiradjuri Land Rights Journey*, 2004, and *Keeping That Good Name*, 2001, written with Evelyn Powell; and for the loan of an SBS video, *Native Title*.

I also want to acknowledge the many articles I read in the *Sydney Morning Herald* and in the *Wellington Times* and on numerous websites, including those of the Native Title Research Unit, the National Native Title Tribunal, NSW

Hansard, NSW State Records, the South Australian Museum's Tinsdale collection, Water Info NSW, Convict Records, the NSW Bureau of Statistics and Crime Research – the analytical work of Don Weatherburn in particular, the online schooling site Skwirk, Agreements, Treaties and Negotiated Settlements (ATNS), the NSW Department of Aboriginal Affairs, and the NSW Department of the Environment, Water, Heritage and the Arts especially their Maynggu Ganai Historic draft conservation management plan.

There are many other people who answered my questions in phone calls, emails and conversations – thank you to all whose names I have not always recorded, but who include officers at Wellington Shire Council; NSW Department of the Environment, Water, Heritage and the Arts; *Wellington Times* Office; Wellington Historical Museum; and the librarian at the Wellington branch of the Macquarie Regional Library.

Thank you to Pamela Freeman and Clare Forster for their invaluable structural comments, Janet Hutchinson for her sensitive editing, and Alexandra Payne at UQP for holding it all together with such grace.

Lastly, let me thank Anthony Reeder for his writing insights, endless support and more trips to the central west than even love has required.